BRITISH ADMIISTRATION IN INDIA

BRITISH ADMIISTRATION IN INDIA

By
G.ANDERSON

GYAN

ISBN : 978-81-212-0146-9

Published, 2018

Published by

Gyan Publishing House
5, Ansari Road
Daryaganj, New Delhi-110002
Phone: 011-47034999, 9811692060
www.gyanbooks.com
E-mail: books@gyanbooks.com

Printed at: G. Print Process, Delhi.

PREFACE

Mr. J. A. R. Marriott has asked the question, whether we do not begin Constitutional History—the history of institutions—at the wrong end, and whether we should start, not with the *Germania* and Stubbs and Dr. Liebermann, but with Mr. Sidney Low and President Lowell, with *Hansard* and *The Times*. The author of this book has also thought—and perhaps the disease may have begun with his attendance at Mr. Marriott's lectures at Oxford many years ago—that lectures to Indian students on English Constitutional History might be more profitable if they dealt with the present-day working of the English Constitution rather than with the Witenagemot, the laws of Ini, or even with the Constitutions of Clarendon. In the meantime, something has been done in this direction in India. In the new courses lately arranged by the Senate of the Bombay University considerable importance has been attached to the study of "Administration." For the Intermediate Examination in Arts the subject of Indian Administration has been prescribed; in the B.A. the Constitution of England, as well as those of Continental Europe as contained in Mr. A. L. Lowell's book, are laid down; and in the M.A. the Administration of the various British Colonies—

a study which we owe very largely to Mr. A. B. Keith —forms a special subject.

The various subjects of study in Indian Administration, as laid down in the University Regulations, were taken very largely from the *Imperial Gazetteer*, but this book, admirable though it may be in many ways, is not suitable as a text-book for Indian students. A somewhat formidable list of authorities, from which the author has extracted much of the material necessary for this work, and to which he owes a debt of gratitude, has been included in these pages, but no single volume covers the whole ground required; and most of these books have been written to expound the methods of British rule in India from a particular point of view, and to prove a particular contention. Such, obviously, is not the type of book required for College students in their second year, who are not expected to criticise or to form opinions as to the working of the various departments of Government. The student requires a mere statement of fact, and the general public an expression of opinion. This book, therefore, is intended solely for the use of students, and not for the general public.

It is with much diffidence that this book has been written. The task has been a difficult one. Each Provincial Government has very largely its own system; changes are always taking place; and even Government Reports are soon out of date. The author, moreover, cannot claim a knowledge of the Government of India in all its branches, and indeed it would be difficult to find anyone who had enjoyed such an experience. A Professor at an Indian College, however holds a somewhat detached and lonely position, and perhaps has less temptation than other Englishmen resident in India to express opinions on these matters. It is possible, therefore, that he has some advantages in writing a book of this nature for Indian students; and, in addition, he is constantly reminded of the fact that he has more leisure than other Government officials in India.

CONTENTS

CHAPTER I.

HISTORICAL INTRODUCTION.

"We seem, as it were, to have conquered and peopled half the world in a fit of absence of mind." SIR JOHN SEELEY.

"The East is a University in which the scholar never takes a degree." LORD CURZON.

"It is not by believing either ourselves or our laws all purity or all corruption that we are likely to come to a right understanding of what is best for India, but by a close study of its past history, and then by setting ourselves down, each in his own sphere, and working out the details of a code honestly and ably prepared, not shifting and changing from day to day, but founded on experience, and suitable to a rude and simple people, who like all people under the sun prefer justice to law."
SIR HENRY LAWRENCE.

"The essence of the 'double government' system was that the substance of authority passed from the Company to the Crown. The Company reigned but in important matters did not govern." SIR T. L. HOLDERNESS.

"THE history of British India falls into three periods. From the beginning of the seventeenth to the middle of the eighteenth century the East India Company is a trading corporation, existing on the sufferance of native powers and in rivalry with the merchant companies of Holland and France. During the next century the Company acquires and consolidates its dominion, shares its sovereignty in increasing proportions with

Division of periods.

the Crown, and gradually loses its mercantile privileges and functions. After the mutiny of 1857 the remaining privileges of the Company are transferred to the Crown, and then follows an era of peace in which India awakens to new life and progress."[1] In following the growth of the Indian Constitution, therefore, we shall notice very briefly in the first place the charters which were given from time to time to the East India Company in the early days of its history; after that, the Acts of Parliament relating to India and the revision of the charter made every twenty years, which tended more and more to limit the powers and privileges of the Company and to increase the responsibility of Parliament over India; and, finally, the Acts of Parliament since 1857 under which the existing constitution of India has mainly been built up.

(1) 1599–1772. **The East India Company.**

Discovery of the New World and growth of modern Europe.

By the capture of Constantinople and the discovery of the New World and of the Cape of Good Hope the history of Europe was altogether changed. The centre of interest shifted from the eastern shores of the Mediterranean to the Atlantic, which became the new Mediterranean of the modern world. The nations of Western Europe, by the assistance of their geographical position and by the venturesome bravery of their sailors, took the lead in opening up the trade of the East as well as of the West. Vasco da Gama landed in Calicut in 1499, and shortly afterwards the Portuguese Empire in the

[1] *Gazetteer*, vol. iv., p. 5.

East was founded. A few years later, Portugal became merged in the greater power of Spain, whose trade monopoly was already being challenged both by England and Holland. In the history of England also this was a time of great importance, when the feebleness of the Lancastrians was replaced by the strong national rule of the Tudors, when the seeds of the union of England and Scotland were being sown, when a national Church was established, and when the foundations of the British Empire were laid. Holland at the same time was engaged in a heroic struggle against the might of Spain, which resulted in her gaining independence from the tyranny of the Spaniard.

It was impossible, therefore, for Spain and Portugal to retain the monopoly of the Eastern trade, and their power soon began to decline.

The Chartered Companies.

The Protestant nations of England and Holland, though for some time on friendly terms in Europe, soon found that their interests clashed in the East, and throughout the seventeenth century their traders competed for the advantage. The position of the individual trader was most perilous; whatever might be the state of international politics in Europe, there was no quarter given on the high seas. The pursuit of trade had to be backed up by armed force, and victory rested with the strong. It was for this reason that Chartered Companies came into existence. About the same time that the Dutch founded an East India Company, Queen Elizabeth granted to certain London merchants a charter for trading purposes in the East Indies, which has been likened to a licence for private war. The relations between the Crown and the Company were left vague, as the State did not wish to be implicated in open warfare with a nation with whom very possibly she might be on friendly terms in Europe. In return for these privileges, which amounted to a trade monopoly so far as England was concerned, the East India Company paid to the Crown from time to time a share of its profits.

Their Development.

The Company thus found it easy to raise large sums of money to pursue its commercial policy in the East, and in an indirect manner built up by degrees that connection between Great Britain and India which at a later period became more intimate. The charter granted by Elizabeth was renewed from time to time by the sovereign, and after the Revolution of 1688 by Act of Parliament. Apart from this, and from taking a share in the profits, the Government of Great Britain took no responsibility in the affairs of the Company. At first the control was placed in a Governor and Council; and at a later date the Courts of Proprietors and Directors were constituted. The qualification for the former was the possession of £500 stock and upwards, and for the latter £2000 stock was necessary. The Directors were elected annually by the Proprietors. The relation between the two Courts was somewhat ill-defined, but apparently the Proprietors could overrule the decisions of the Directors. Besides the trade monopoly, the Company had under their charter the right "to acquire territory, fortify their stations, defend their property by armed force, coin money and administer justice within their own settlements." Though the Dutch and the Portuguese soon went beyond the mere pursuit of trade, and began to seize territory as opportunity offered, the English at first sought trading facilities rather than possessions, and were thus content with a few trading stations. The first of these was at Surat, where certain concessions were granted by the Emperor Jehangir. In 1616, the Company opened a factory at Masulipatam, and in 1640 Fort St. George was built at Madras on land bought from an Indian ruler. A factory was also built on the Hugli, which in 1690 was moved to Calcutta ; and in 1662 the Portuguese handed over Bombay to Charles II., who granted it a few years later to the Company "in free and common socage as of the Manor of East Greenwich, on payment of the annual rent of £10."

The Company becomes a political power in India.

At the beginning of the eighteenth century India was in a state of absolute confusion. Aurangzeb, the last of the great Moghuls, died in the year 1707, but even before that time the Muhammadan Empire had shown signs of decay. The Mahratta powers, the Muhammadan princes, and the Hindu rulers were eagerly competing for those territories which had once been included under the rule of the Great Moghul. The security of British trade therefore was in danger, and it became impossible for the Company to cease from interference in Indian politics. The Dutch, mainly owing to their misfortunes at home, had declined in power, and had retired to the East Indies, where their rule still prevails. In the meantime, another European power had entered the lists. It was in 1664, during the long reign of Louis XIV., that the French East

India Company was founded under the fostering care of Colbert, but by the futility and folly of his European wars, by the persecution of the Huguenots, the most industrious of his subjects, and by the over-centralization of his government, Louis sowed the seeds of future trouble and also checked the progress of French enterprise in the East. It was not until the eighteenth century was well advanced and Louis himself was dead that the fortunes of France in the East began to improve. In 1715, Mauritius was captured, and became the head-quarters of the French fleet in Eastern waters; and Pondicherry and Chandernagore became starting-points for fresh adventures on the mainland. The arrival of Dupleix as Governor of Pondicherry in 1741 proved a turning-point in Indian history. He realized to the full the possibilities that awaited the successful European power in India. It was his policy to take part in the rivalries between the native princes, and to discipline Indian troops after the European fashion. His success was immediate; and France became for a time the dominating power in Southern India. The brilliant generalship of Clive, however, the heart-rending neglect shown by the French Government at home, and, above all, British control of the sea, proved fatal to the ambitions of Dupleix, and both in Bengal and Southern India the East India Company found itself forced to accept responsibilities far beyond what had ever been anticipated. In 1765, Clive accepted in the name of the Company the Diwani of Bengal, Bihar, and Orissa from the Emperor at Delhi, and with that memorable event the first period may be said to end.

(2) 1772–1858. Double Government.

In 1772, when Lord North's ministry was in power, the eyes of England were turned to India, where an altogether novel position had arisen. A trading company had been forced by peculiar circumstances to take part in Indian politics, and assume responsibilities of government over millions of people. Public opinion in England was largely mistaken as to the real state of affairs in India. It was true that some servants of the Company were amassing for themselves gigantic fortunes, but at the same time the finances of the Company were at a very low ebb. The debts were large; the need of maintaining a standing army was imperative; its arms were not always successful, Hyder Ali having just won a signal victory over the Company's troops in the south; and famine had reduced the province of Bengal to abject poverty. Yet all the time large dividends were being paid, and the holders of stock were clamouring for more. Moreover, stories of oppression were constantly being brought from the East. Many thought that the only solution of the difficulty was that the British Government should take a more active share in the management of the Company's property, and that the political powers of the Company should be defined as clearly as possible.

To meet these difficulties the Regulating Act was passed. The immediate and more pressing financial difficulties of the Company were relieved, and regulations were made to prevent the payment of excessive dividends. But Lord North's Government dealt with matters far more important than the imminent bankruptcy of the

Regulating Act, 1772.

East India Company, and took into consideration the whole question of Company rule in India. At home the constitution of the Courts of Directors and Proprietors was changed. The Directors' tenure of office was increased from one to four years; and the right of voting in the Court of Proprietors was restricted to those who had held stock amounting to £1000 for at least twelve months. In India the responsibility to make and issue rules, alliances, and regulations for the good order and civil government was handed over to the Governor-General of Bengal assisted by three councillors, who also had supervisory powers over the Governments of Madras and Bombay. The appointment of Warren Hastings, the first Governor-General, and of his councillors was included in the Act, but after a period of five years the Indian patronage was to return to the directors. The Act also provided for the constitution of a Supreme Court at Calcutta. Sir Elijah Impey was the first Chief Justice, and he was assisted by three judges.

Fox's East India Bill.

The passing of the Regulating Act was the first event of importance in this second period which saw a system of "Double Government" established in India, in which the responsibilities were shared by the Crown and the Company. Within a few years it became obvious that affairs in India were still by no means satisfactory. Hastings' rule, which had lasted for ten years, had been full of difficulties. Hyder Ali in the south, and the Mahrattas in the west had been in alliance with the French, and it was only with the greatest danger and with enormous expense that Hastings had been able to maintain the British position in India. Moreover, there had been violent quarrels between the Governor-General and certain members of his Council; and there were still stories of oppression towards the peoples of India. The Coalition Ministry of Fox and North was then in office, and the former decided to deal with the problems in India. In 1783, he introduced his East India Bill before the House of Commons. The solution of the difficulty appeared to him to lie in the extension of the power of the Crown over the Government in India. For this purpose seven Commissioners, named in the Bill, were to be appointed, who should control the management of Indian affairs. The regulation of commerce was to be entrusted to nine Directors appointed by Parliament from amongst the largest Proprietors. William Pitt led the opposition to the Bill, the chief danger of which consisted in the transference of the Indian patronage from the directors to the King's ministers. George III. and his friends had already used the English patronage to organize a party in Parliament, which was bound to them by ties of gratitude, and many viewed with alarm the possibility of the Indian patronage being used for similar purposes. The Bill was eventually thrown out by the House of Lords, and Fox and North were called upon to resign.

When Pitt came into power after the overthrow of the Coalition he found it necessary to frame a Bill for the better government of India.

Pitt's India Act.

He was careful not to repeat the mistakes of Fox, and left the patronage and all matters connected with trade in the hands of the Directors. On the main principles, however, his policy was similar to that of Fox. The guiding hand in future was to be the British Parliament rather than the Company. A Board of Control consisting of six Commissioners was appointed under the Act. Their duties were "to superintend, direct, and control all acts, operations, and concerns which in any wise relate to the Civil and Military Government or revenues of the British territorial possessions in the East Indies." The Chancellor of the Exchequer and one of the Secretaries of State had seats on the Board, but the next senior member became known as the President of the Board of Control. His position was one of great importance, and somewhat similar to that now held by the Secretary of State for India. The Court of Proprietors had refused to sanction the recall of Hastings, though it had been demanded both by the Directors and by the House of Commons. Their powers, therefore, were reduced, and their Court was made subordinate to that of the Directors, whose decisions they had henceforth no power to alter. Pitt's Act, except for a few alterations in detail, remained in force until the year 1858.

Renewal of the Charter.

In 1793, when the time arrived to renew the old charter, Pitt's most intimate friend Dundas was President of the Board of Control. Much detail work was done, and in that year the Covenanted Civil Service was constituted. In 1813, more important questions demanded solution. Much had happened in India. Vast additions had been made to the territory administered by the Company, owing to the successful campaigns of Lord Wellesley; and it was felt that a trade monopoly was unsuitable at a time when other merchants were demanding a share in the profitable trade of the East. The Company fought hard to retain its commercial privileges. The majority of experienced Indian administrators, including Warren Hastings himself, who had long since retired, dealt with the gravity of the situation which might arise as a result of unrestricted trading. There had been much difficulty even in the past, they pointed out, in supervising the relations between the Company's servants and the Indians. In the end a compromise was effected. The Company lost its commercial privileges, but was allowed to retain its monopoly of the tea trade and of that with China ; and a system of licences was made to safeguard the Indians against the wiles of the irresponsible English adventurer. The patronage of the Company and its political privileges were preserved, except that the appointment of the chief officers was made subject to the approval of the Crown.

At the renewal of the charter in 1833, the Company lost its monopoly of the China and the tea trades, which had been preserved on the previous occasion. Though it had thus lost its commercial privileges, the Company still retained its political responsibilities. The wording of the 1853 charter, however, showed clearly that the days of Company rule were numbered in that no fixed time for its duration was mentioned.

(3) 1858. India under the Crown.

The system of Double Government came to an end in 1858, when the Government of India was transferred from the Company to the Crown. The Board of Control was replaced by a Secretary of

State assisted by a Council, in whom was vested the patronage of the more important posts. The Rules and Regulations for the conduct of the Civil Service, as passed in 1853, were continued until 1861, when the Civil Service Act was passed. A list of appointments, reserved for members of the Covenanted Service, was drawn up, though in exceptional cases men outside the service could be appointed subject to the approval of the Secretary of State in Council. The Indian Government was left very largely as it was.

Important Acts of Parliament.

Since 1858 very few Acts of first-rate importance have been passed by the British Parliament with reference to India. Power has been given to increase the size of the Governor-General's Council; new provinces have been formed and existing boundaries have been modified; and the regulations for the Civil Service have, from time to time, been altered. The Indian Councils Act of 1861 put the legislature on a new basis, and restored to the Governments of Madras and Bombay the right of legislation, subject to certain reservations; and arrangements were made for a Legislative Council in Bengal, the North-Western or United Provinces, and the Punjab. Further developments were made in the Indian legislatures under the Act of 1892. In 1861 the judicature was put on a less complicated basis by the High Courts Act, when the Crown and Company Courts were abolished, and High Courts were established at Calcutta, Madras, and Bombay.

The Indian Councils Act of 1909 was introduced before the House of Lords by Lord Morley, and has had a far-reaching effect on the Indian Constitution. The system of "Council Government" was extended by the enlargement of the Executive Councils in Bombay and Madras, where the opportunity was taken of appointing an Indian, and authority was also given to constitute a similar Council in any province where there was a Lieutenant-Governor and in Bengal. The Legislative Councils, both Imperial and Provincial, were considerably enlarged, and the elective element was increased.

Councils Act of 1909.

In 1911, His Majesty King George V., accompanied by the Queen-Empress, visited India for the purpose of holding in person an Imperial Durbar at Delhi. The occasion was unique in the history of India, this being the first time that an English sovereign has landed on Indian soil. The Durbar had a further significance in that the King-Emperor made proclamations of great importance. The capital of India, which had been for many years at Calcutta, was to be removed to Delhi, a city of many historic memories; and a re-arrangement of certain provinces was also adopted. In the following year, a Bill was introduced before Parliament by which some of these changes were carried into effect.

The Durbar of 1911.

Such, then, is a brief introduction to the study of the Indian Constitution and the history of its administration. The chief Acts of Parliament relating to India have been mentioned, and it is unnecessary at present to speak of others of lesser importance. It must be clearly understood, however, that it is subject to these Acts passed by the British Parliament that the government of India is carried on. The Executive, the Legislature, and the Judicature of India are constituted in accordance with them ; and alterations in, and amendments of, these Acts can only be made through the British Parliament.

CHAPTER II.

THE SECRETARY OF STATE FOR INDIA AND HIS COUNCIL.

"In England there are no two parties about India. It is the desire of all parties that the Government of this dependency should be conducted with insight and sympathy, and that our guiding stars should be mercy and justice." LORD CURZON.

The Court of Directors and the Board of Control.

IN the foregoing pages it has been seen that Pitt's Act of 1784 established a dual authority, whereby the controlling power over the Government of India was shared between the Court of Directors representing the Company, and the Board of Control representing the Crown. The Directors were elected by those who had held a certain amount of stock for twelve months or more, and the members of the Board of Control were nominated by the Crown. The Board originally consisted of six members, but in the course of time the number was reduced, and after 1841 the President became the only member. The balance of power was in the hands of the Board, whose responsibilities were increased as time went on. The Directors could not send a dispatch to India without submitting it first to the Board, and, in addition, the Board could insist on a dispatch being prepared by the Directors on any subject it pleased.

The Secretary of State and his Council.

In 1858, when the Crown assumed the sole responsibility for the government of India, the office of the President of the Board of Control was replaced by that of a fifth Secretary of State, who was assisted by a Council. The Secretary of State for India is a member of Parliament, a Cabinet Minister, and a member of the Privy Council. He must, therefore, have the support of a majority in the House of Commons, and accepts or resigns office according to the exigencies of party government in England. The members of the Council, on the other hand, hold a position vitally different from that of the Secretary of State. They are debarred by statute from holding a seat in Parliament, and thus take no active share in party politics. There were originally fifteen Councillors in all, but the Council now consists "of such number of members, not less than ten and not more than fourteen, as the Secretary of State may from time to time determine." They are appointed by the Secretary of State, and hold office during good behaviour. They can only be removed by an address passed through both Houses. The term of office was originally for ten, but has recently been reduced to seven years. A certain proportion of the members must have served or resided in British India for not less than seven years, and not left British India more than five years before the date of their appointment. At present, two of the members are Indians, one a Hindu and the other a Muhammadan. The Council, therefore, is very complete, retired civil servants,

Indians, military experts, financiers, and educationists all being represented. The Council is divided into committees, which meet on certain days of the week, and supervise the work of the various departments.

The Secretary of State is the President of the Council. The Vice-President is appointed by the Secretary of State, who has the power to remove him at any time. The Council has powers of supervision only over those matters which are placed before it by the Secretary of State, and has no initiative authority whatever. Besides, the Secretary of State may overrule his Council except in certain cases, such as the appropriation of revenues or property, alteration of salaries and furlough rules, and the appointment of Indians to posts reserved for the Covenanted Civil Service, where a majority of votes on the Council is necessary. In the event of a disagreement between members of the Council and the Secretary of State, any member who has been present at the meeting may claim the right of recording in the minutes his disapproval of the steps taken and the reasons for his action. Except in cases of urgency and secrecy, all orders and dispatches must either be discussed at a meeting of the Council, or be open for inspection in the Council-room for at least seven days before being sent to India. Broadly speaking, therefore, the powers of the Council are only of an advisory nature. Indirectly, however, its influence may be very considerable. Although men such as Lord Lansdowne, Lord Northbrook, and Lord Ripon, have been members of the Cabinet, no Secretary of State for

Relations between the Secretary of State and his Council.

India as yet has previously held office in India. He is, therefore, lacking in experience of the affairs he is called upon to administer, and must necessarily be influenced very considerably by the opinions of those members of his Council, English and Indian, who have spent the better part of their lives in the service of India.

Powers of the Secretary of State.

"The Secretary of State [1] is the constitutional adviser of the Crown in all matters relating to India. He inherits generally all the powers and duties which were formerly vested either in the Board of Control, or in the Company, the Directors, and the Secret Committee in respect of the government and revenues of India. He has the power of giving orders to every officer in India, including the Governor-General, and of directing all the business relating to the Government of India that is transacted in the United Kingdom. Every order or communication sent to India must be signed by him or, in his absence, by some other Secretary of State, and every dispatch from India must likewise be addressed to him. Of these wide powers and duties many rest on his personal responsibility; others can be performed only in consultation with his Council, and for some of these the concurrence of a majority of members of Council is required." His Majesty acts on his advice in making the appointments which are reserved to the Crown, except that of the Viceroy, who is recommended by the Prime Minister. Legally speaking, therefore, the powers of the Secretary of State are very wide. What they are in practice is more difficult to determine. Only

[1] *Gazetteer*, vol. iv. p. 36.

those who have had an intimate experience both in the Indian and Home Governments can answer such questions, and doubtless much depends upon the character of the man put in control. Sir John Strachey, who was a member of the Government of India under five Viceroys, and was afterwards a member of the India Council in London, has perhaps a right equal to that of any other to give an opinion on this point. "The action of the Secretary of State," he says, "is mainly confined to answering references made to him by the Government of India, and, apart from great political and financial questions, the number and nature of these references mainly depend on the character of the Governor-General for the time being. Some men in that position like to minimise personal responsibilities, and to ask for the orders of the Home Government before taking any action. Others prefer to act on their own judgment and on that of their Councillors. *The Secretary of State in ordinary times initiates little.* So long as the Government of India is content to carry on the administration without largely increasing the cost of existing establishments, and without incurring new and heavy charges, it is practically almost independent, so far as its action in the internal affairs of India is concerned."[1] Even if this opinion be taken as correct, the Home Government plays a big part in the Government of India. The same writer has pointed out that, owing to climatic and other reasons, there is frequent change in the personnel of the administration, and that the Viceroy, the Governors, Lieutenant-Governors, and members of their Councils rarely hold office for more

[1] *India: Its Administration and Progress*, Strachey, p. 76.

than five years. Some degree of continuity of policy is essential in every government, and all the more in a country such as India, where the people are disinclined to sudden and violent changes. It is in this respect that the Secretary of State and his Council can and do exert a salutary influence.

Patronage of the Secretary of State.

Originally, as has been seen, the question of Indian appointments was the rock on which the Coalition of Fox and North was wrecked; and Pitt wisely decided to leave the Indian patronage in the hands of the Company. In 1813, the appointment of the Governor-General, the Governors, and the Commander-in-Chief was made subject to the approval of the Crown.

India Office.

At the present day the patronage at the disposal of the Secretary of State is not great, even in his own office at Westminster. He is assisted there by two Under-Secretaries, the one a Government official and the other a member of Parliament. The latter is a member of the Government, and holds office only for so long as his party remains in power. In 1858 the servants of the Board of Control and of the Court of Directors were re-engaged by the Secretary of State in the service of his establishment known as the India Office. Admission to the upper-division clerkships is now regulated by the same rules and examinations as those for the Indian and Colonial services. The lower grade posts, known as second-division clerkships and assistant clerkships, are filled by successful candidates in other competitive examinations. Within the office itself all appointments and promotions are settled by the Secretary of State in Council, except that of the auditor, who

India Office appointments.

is appointed by the Crown by a warrant countersigned by the Chancellor of the Exchequer. The salaries, pensions, and other charges of the India Office are paid from the revenues of India.

Indian appointments.

The Secretary of State has comparatively little to do with Indian appointments. The Governor-General is appointed by the Crown acting on the advice of the Prime Minister, but the Commander-in-Chief, the Governors, and Members of Council are appointed by the Crown acting on the advice of the Secretary of State. Lieutenant-Governors are appointed by the Crown acting on the advice of the Governor-General. The rules under which the judges of the High Court are appointed will be explained later. With regard to important posts below that of a member of Council two things should be noted. In 1793 was constituted what was known as the Covenanted Civil Service, the members of which entered into covenants with the East India Company, binding themselves not to receive presents or to take part in trade; and for members of this service certain posts were reserved. Admission to this service was gained by the nomination of the Directors until 1853, when the competitive system was introduced. The service was then made open to all British subjects, irrespective of race, caste, or religion. The regulations with regard to the age and qualifications of the candidates, and the subjects prescribed for the examination, are made by the Secretary of State in Council, and any alterations in them must first be laid before Parliament. The examination itself is conducted by the Civil Service Commissioners. The system, on the whole, has worked admirably. All questions of appointments and promotions are left entirely to the Government of India; and by this means the Civil Service is freed from the baneful influences of party politics, and from charges of nepotism and favouritism.

In past years, however, the system has caused some dissatisfaction in one respect. The number of Indians in the Indian Civil Service has been and still is very small. The fact that the examination is held in London has prevented some from entering the service. In 1879, the Statutory Civil Service was instituted, which was open to Indians of proved merit and ability, who were nominated by the Local Governments, subject to the approval of the Secretary of State in Council. This new system did not prove a success, and in 1887 another arrangement was made in accordance with the suggestions made by the Public Service Commission, presided over by Sir Charles Aitchison, the Lieutenant-Governor of the Punjab. The Government service was then and still is divided into three divisions—The Indian Civil Service, The Provincial Service, and The Subordinate Service. Admission to the Provincial and Subordinate Services is in accordance with the rules and regulations laid down by the local Governments, and is usually by nomination from candidates possessing the necessary qualifications. Members of the Subordinate Service are eligible for promotion to the Provincial Service, and members of the Provincial Service are eligible for certain 'listed' posts formerly reserved for the Indian Civil Service.[1]

Indians and the Public services.

[1] In the Bombay Presidency there are two posts of Collectors, and one post of Talukdari Settlement Office on the Revenue

There are certain other services in India, such as the Public Works, Telegraphs, Forests, Police, Education and the Medical, and in each of these are similar divisions. The Imperial Service is recruited in England, in some cases by examination, and in others by nomination of the Secretary of State. The majority of those appointed are Europeans, but Indians are eligible, and have been selected. The Provincial and Subordinate Services are recruited in India under rules prescribed by the local Governments.

Other services.

In 1912, a Public Services Commission was appointed by Royal Warrant under the Chairmanship of Lord Islington, who had recently been Governor of New Zealand, to inquire into the methods of recruitment, the conditions of service, the working of the existing systems of division of the services into Imperial and Provincial, and generally to consider the requirements of the public services.

Public Services Commission, 1912.

There is yet to be considered the relationship between the Secretary of State and Parliament. The position of the Secretary of State for India is different from that of the Secretary of State for the Colonies. The salaries of the latter and of his establishment form a charge on the Home Government, and are therefore included in the estimates placed before the House of Commons every year. When these items are under discussion, there can be a debate

The Secretary of State and Parliament.

Side, and two posts of District and Sessions Judges, three posts of Assistant Judges and one post of Registrar of the High Court on the Judicial Side, which used to be held by members of the Indian Civil Service, and are now open to members of the Provincial Service.

on the general policy of the Colonial Secretary or any details connected with his work, and alterations in his estimates may be made by the House of Commons. This is not the case with the Secretary of State for India, whose salary is a charge on the Indian and not on the Home Exchequer. The revenues and expenditure of India, therefore, are not subject to parliamentary correction, except that no increase in the public debt of India and no expenditure to meet the expenses of military operations beyond the frontier may be made without the consent of Parliament. A financial statement, commonly known as the Indian Budget, and audited by an independent auditor, showing the revenues and expenditure of the past year, and a detailed report of the material and moral progress of British India, are submitted to Parliament every year, but these statements are only followed by a formal resolution, setting forth the actual revenue and expenditure in India.

Acts of Parliament and the Indian Administration.

In the last chapter certain Acts of Parliament were mentioned which define and legalize the executive, the legislature, and the judicature of India. No alterations can be made in these Acts without the consent of Parliament. On the other hand, changes of vast importance, which are not governed by previous Acts of Parliament, such as the transfer of the capital from Calcutta to Delhi need not be submitted to Parliament at all. The recent appointment of Indian non-officials to the Executive Councils may make this distinction clear. Only a certain proportion of the members of the Governor-General's Council need have served under the Crown in India, and thus a non-official Indian could be appointed by the Secretary of State without any alterations in the existing statute. The Councils of Madras and Bombay, on the other hand, consisted each of two members besides the Governor, both of them were bound by statute to have served the Crown in India for a certain length of time. An alteration in the statute, therefore, being necessary, reference had to be made to Parliament before a non-official of any race could be appointed.

The Secretary of State also is a member of the Cabinet, and as such is responsible to Parliament. Questions concerning the Government of India may therefore be asked in either House, and it is open to any member, subject to the rules of the House, to promote a discussion and to submit a resolution. At the present day the House of Lords takes a keener interest in Indian affairs than the House of Commons; this is probably due to the inclusion in the House of Lords of many ex-Viceroys and Governors and men possessed of considerable Indian experience.

In conclusion, the Secretary of State has very wide powers over the Government of India, but in practice it appears that his functions are, to a large extent, of an advisory or corrective nature. Again, though the sovereignty of Parliament over India is clearly established, the occasions when Parliament interferes in Indian affairs are comparatively few. It is fortunate, perhaps, that for many years the administration of India has been removed from the vortex of party politics in England. Lord Morley's reforms were considered beyond the scope of party politics, and were accepted by both the great political parties in England. The Government of India, therefore, is in the main responsible for the management of Indian affairs, subject to the supervision of the Secretary of State and, in some cases, of the British Parliament.

CHAPTER III.

THE VICEROY AND HIS COUNCIL.

"Never let it be forgotten that the Government of India is governed not by an individual, but by a committee. No important act can be taken without the assent of a majority of that committee."
LORD CURZON.

"The Viceroy is the leading member of the Indian Government, but he is only one of several members. Lord Mayo used to fight hard officially for his views, and, as a matter of fact, he got more of his own way than most Governors-General have done. But he was essentially loyal to his colleagues and upon all points on which they beat him or on which he once yielded, he forthwith accepted the joint action of the Government as his own."
SIR WILLIAM HUNTER.

The Governor-General.

BY the terms of the Regulating Act the Governor of Bengal was made Governor-General with controlling powers over the Governments of Madras and Bombay; and his authority was extended under Pitt's Act of 1784, and again in 1793. In 1833, the title of Governor-General of India was substituted for that of Governor-General of Bengal, but it was not until 1854 that the Governor-General was relieved of the direct responsibility for the Government of Bengal on the appointment of a Lieutenant-Governor for that province. From that time onwards the Government of India has ceased to be connected with any particular province. Its headquarters continued to be at Calcutta, though since the time of Lord Lawrence it has been customary for the Governor-General and the chief officers of his Government to reside at Simla during the summer months. In 1912, the capital was removed from Calcutta to Delhi, which town and the surrounding country were placed under the direct control of the Government of India. In 1858, when the Government of India was transferred from the Company to the Crown, the Governor-General became known as the Viceroy, but in parliamentary documents the term Governor-General is still used. Originally the Governor-General was appointed by the Directors, but in 1813 the approval of the Crown became necessary. To-day, he is appointed by the Crown, acting on the advice of the Prime Minister; and the term of office is usually for five years. It has been laid down that the Governor-General should obey all such orders as he may receive from the Secretary of State. Apart from this restriction, his powers are very large. He is the representative of the Crown in India, the head of the administration, and the president of the legislature; and in him are placed the prerogatives of mercy and pardon.

Under the Regulating Act the Governor-General was assisted by a Council of four members. The members of the Council were originally selected by the Directors, but are now appointed by the Crown, acting on the advice of the Secretary of State, and usually hold office for a period of five years. The size of the Council has changed from time to time. Pitt's Act provided for a Council of three members, one of whom was to

His Council.

be the Commander-in-Chief. In 1912, the Governor-General's Council consisted of six members, and, in addition, the Commander-in-Chief sat on the Council as an extraordinary member. The qualifications necessary for membership of the Council are important. Three of the members must by statute have been engaged in the service of the Crown in India for ten years or more at the time of their appointment; and another must be a barrister of England or Ireland or a member of the Faculty of Advocates of Scotland of not less than five years standing. In 1912, three members belonged to the Indian Civil Service; two had been members of the Civil Service in London, and had not previously been connected with Indian official life; and the sixth was an Indian barrister possessed of the necessary qualifications.

Relations between the Governor-General and members of his Council.

Warren Hastings, the first Governor-General, was continually thwarted by the opposition of a majority on his Council, who used their power of overruling him on several occasions. To-day, the Governor-General is bound to abide by the decision of the majority on his Council, except on such matters as in his opinion concern "the safety, tranquillity, or interests of British India." This privilege is rarely used, but it is worthy of note that Lord Lytton was forced to overrule his Council on the question of the tariff. In such cases the dissenting member has the right to record the reasons for his disagreement, which are forwarded to the Secretary of State. The methods of "Council Government" have changed very much in recent times. In the olden days all matters connected with the administration were discussed by the Council. "The system involved," says a former member of Council, "an amount of elaborate minute writing, which seems now hardly conceivable. Twenty years ago the Governor-General and his Council used to perform work which now would be disposed of by an Under-Secretary." Lord Dalhousie, whose time was engaged in the consideration of many matters of vast importance, came to the conclusion that the Governor-General could not possibly continue to work under such a system, and the Councils Act of 1861 permitted the Governor-General to make such rules and regulations as seemed to him necessary for the more convenient transaction of business. In accordance with this clause, Lord Canning assigned to each member of his Council the charge of a department, in the ordinary business of which he became the responsible chief: Matters of importance, however, are reserved for discussion at a meeting of the Council. In his *Life of Lord Mayo*, Sir William Hunter has given the following description of the way in which the work of the Council is carried out :

"Routine and ordinary matters were disposed of by the members of Council within whose department they fell. Papers of greater importance were sent, with the initiating member's opinion, to the Viceroy, who either concurred in or modified it. If the Viceroy concurred, the case generally ended, and the Secretary worked up the member's note into a letter or a resolution, to be issued as the orders of the Governor-General in Council. But in matters of weight, the Viceroy, even when concurring with the initiating member, often directed the papers to be circulated either to the whole Council, or to certain of the members whose views he might think it expedient to obtain on the question. In cases in which he did not concur with the initiating member's views, the papers were generally circulated to all other members, or the Governor-General ordered them to be brought up in Council. Urgent business was submitted to the Governor-General direct by the Secretary of the Department under which it fell; and the Viceroy either initiated the order himself, or sent the case for initiation to the Member of Council at the Head of the Department to which it belonged."

Foreign Department.

The Foreign Department is under the direct supervision of the Governor-General himself. The Foreign Office supervises the Governments of the Native States in a varying degree. [1] "The maximum of sovereignty enjoyed by any of the rulers of the native states is represented by a prince like the Nizam of Hyderabad, who coins money, taxes his subjects, and inflicts punishment without appeal. The minimum of sovereignty is represented by a lord of a few acres in Kathiawar, who enjoys immunity from British taxation and exercises some shadow of individual authority." The representatives of the Foreign Office in Native States are known as Residents or Agents, and are selected usually from members of the Indian Civil Service or from military officers who are members of the Political Department. The supervision of such matters connected with the native states as the Chiefs' Colleges and the Imperial Service Troops also rests with this office. The Foreign Department also assumes control of the

[1] Ilbert, *The Government of India*, p. 139.

North-West Frontier Province, Ajmer-Merwara, and British Baluchistan.

The Home Department. and Education. The Home Department controls the general administration of British India, but in 1910 a new Member of Council was appointed to supervise the important departments of education and sanitation.

Revenue and Agriculture. The Department of Revenue and Agriculture deals very largely with questions connected with the land. As will be seen later, a large portion of the Indian revenues is derived from the land in the shape of land revenue or rent, which is paid to the Government. It is the work of this department to supervise the collection of this money, and to see that the assessments are made on the best and most equitable basis. Another important duty is to supervise the arrangements made by the Local Governments for famine relief, and also to encourage as far as possible the development of scientific agriculture. The management of Public Works also comes under the supervision of this department.

Law Member. In 1833, arrangements were made for the appointment of a new member of Council, and in the following year Macaulay arrived in India as the first Law Member. The duties of this official are to assist in the drafting of Bills which are to be submitted to the Legislative Council, to preside over select committees appointed to consider in detail any Bill that may be committed to them by the Legislative Council, and also to advise the Government on all matters connected with legal affairs.

In a later chapter it will be seen that many of

the functions of the Finance Member have been delegated to the provincial, municipal, and local authorities, but he still retains powers of supervision over all matters of finance, and he still keeps the entire management of certain departments in his own hands. Matters connected with the defence forces of the Empire, the public debt, the mint, customs, tribute from native states, post office and telegraphs and opium are under the management of the central authority. The necessary supervision over the financial arrangements of the provincial and local authorities is maintained by the provincial Accountants-General and their officers, who are responsible to the Comptroller and Auditor-General.

Finance Member.

In years past the Government of India was somewhat out of touch with the commercial world, and "a barrier of mistrust on the one hand and of contempt on the other hand had arisen between the commercial and official circles." Lord Curzon "was the first Viceroy to make it thoroughly clear to business men that he meant to help them, and that he regarded them as an integral part of the fabric of the Indian Empire." The Chambers of Commerce in the different business centres have afforded some means by which the Government can find out the views of business people on matters connected with the trade of the country, but Lord Curzon's Government went further in the institution of a new department of Commerce and Industry to the Head of which a seat on the Executive Council was given. His duties are manifold. The supervision of all industrial projects in India, the collection and dis-

Commerce and Industry.

tribution of commercial intelligence, the management of the post office and telegraphs, customs, ports and merchant shipping, mining and factories are all committed to his charge. The control of the railways and the development of a railway policy was at the same time handed over to a Railway Board, consisting of three members, who are represented on the Viceroy's Council by the Member for Commerce and Industry. The department is also expected to regulate the trade of the country, and to interfere, when necessary, in the interests of health and humanity. The inspection of labour and factories was formerly somewhat slack, and consequently a Bill was passed by the Imperial Council insisting upon the limitation of the hours of work, a more efficient inspection of factories, and provisions preventing women and young children doing certain kinds of work.

Secretariat Officials.

At the head of each department is the Member, and below him are the Secretary, the Under and the Assistant Secretaries, and the ordinary clerical establishments. The Assistant Secretary and the subordinate staff are men permanently connected with the department. Except in the Public Works Department the Secretaries and the Under-Secretaries are members of the Indian Civil Service. The Government of India has no special Civil Service of its own, but the services of officers serving under the Provincial Governments are borrowed by the Government of India, and the period for holding secretariat appointments under the Government of India is usually limited to three years.

The Government of India is what may be called

a unitary and not a federal Government. In its relations with other Indian authorities, its power is supreme and undivided, and the Local Governments act as its agents. In other words, the Local Governments perform certain duties which are entrusted to them by the Government of India. This has not always been the case, as in the olden days the Governments of Madras and Bombay were independent of that of Bengal. The Australian Constitution provides an example of a federal Government. In consequence of their geographical position and of their historical past, the States have been in favour of preserving, as far as possible, the autonomy of each and of avoiding undue centralization. The Central or Federal Government of the Commonwealth of Australia only possesses certain powers, which are strictly defined in the Commonwealth Act, whilst all those powers not mentioned therein are retained by the States. In South Africa the unitary form of government has lately been adopted. Almost all power is now concentrated in the Union Government, and the Provincial Councils have only a limited legislative and executive authority. The Canadian Constitution stands midway between those of Australia and South Africa. In that country the Dominion Parliament possesses all powers, except those definitely handed over to the Provincial Governments.

Government of India, a unitary government.

The Government of India administers all matters relating to foreign affairs, the defences of the country, general taxation, currency, debt, tariff, posts and telegraphs, railways, and auditing of accounts. Ordinary internal administration, such as police, civil and criminal justice, prisons, the assessment and collection of the revenues, education, medical and sanitary arrangements, buildings and roads, forests, and the control over municipal and district boards fall to the share of the Provincial Governments. But even in these matters the Government of India exercises a general and constant control. They lay down the lines of general policy, and test their application from the administration reports and returns relating to the departments under the Local Governments. They also employ expert officers to inspect and advise upon a number of departments, which are primarily administered by the Local Governments. The tendency of recent times, however, has been to abolish the posts held by the Inspectors-General, as they are called.

Decentralization.

During recent years a policy of decentralization has been adopted, which in all probability will be extended still further in the near future. In 1907 the Royal Commission upon Decentralization in India was appointed under the chairmanship of Mr. Hobhouse. One of its members was Mr. Romesh Chunder Dutt, a retired civil servant, who had been a Commissioner in Bengal, and was at the time acting as Diwan in the Baroda State. The findings of the Commission and the evidence of witnesses are published in a big volume, which affords most interesting reading to the student of Indian administration. Various suggestions were made, many of which are gradually being carried into effect. As to the merits of the policy of Decentralization, Sir John Strachey speaks very strongly. "The policy of the Government of India is not to interfere unnecessarily with the details of provincial administration. The fact is recognized that the provincial governments possess more knowledge of local requirements and conditions than any in which the distant authorities of the central government can pretend." [1]

CHAPTER IV.

PROVINCIAL GOVERNMENTS.

"What you want is to decentralise your Government. You will not make a single step towards the improvement of India unless you change your whole system of Government—unless you give to each Presidency a Government with more independent powers than are now possessed." JOHN BRIGHT.

"The Government of India has supreme and undivided authority, subject, of course, to the home Government. It is a unitary and not a federal Government. The local Governments are its agents, and they derive their various powers from it." SIR T. W. HOLDERNESS.

"Invested as you are with all the powers of Government over all parts of India, and responsible for good Government in them all, you are to consider to what extent, and in what particulars, the powers of Government can be best exercised by the local authorities, and to what extent, or in what particulars, they are likely to be best exercised when retained in your own hands."
DISPATCH FROM COURT OF DIRECTORS TO THE GOVERNMENT OF INDIA, 1834.

"Future policy should be directed to steadily enlarging the spheres of detailed administration entrusted to Provincial Governments and the authorities subordinate to them, and of recognizing that they must definitely dispose of an increasing share in the ordinary work of Government."
REPORT OF THE DECENTRALIZATION COMMITTEE.

Provincial Governments.

BRITISH India is divided into provinces, each being controlled by its own Local Government, which must obey the orders of the Governor-General in Council. As has been noticed already, the army, the posts and telegraphs, the railways, and such departments as require a uniform policy are kept under the direct control and management of the Government of India, and with these the Provincial Governments have no concern. A certain proportion of the revenue is handed over to the Local Government, the basis of which is arranged by a settlement extending over a certain number of years. The Provincial Governments manage certain departments, such as those of education, police, hospitals and sanitation, and ordinary public works, subject merely to the general control of the Government of India. The Local Governments differ from each other in the extent of their powers, those of Madras, Bombay, and Bengal naturally having the greatest amount of independence. In 1912 there were the following fourteen provinces:

1. The Presidencies or Governorships of Madras, Bombay, and Bengal.
2. The Lieutenant-Governorships of the United Provinces of Agra and Oudh, the Punjab, Burma, and Bihar and Orissa.
3. The Chief Commissionerships of the Central Provinces, Assam, and North-West Frontier Province.
4. British Baluchistan, Ajmer-Merwara, Coorg and the Andaman Isles.

Regulation and Non-regulation provinces.

In the olden days there was a wide distinction between what were known as the "Regulation" and "Non-regulation" provinces. The former consisted of Bengal, Madras, Bombay, and Agra, the remaining provinces including Oudh and Sind, being termed "Non-regulation." The Regulation provinces were administered under "Regulations" or laws passed by the Government in accordance with the Charter Acts, but it was found that a different system of government was necessary for the less advanced districts, which had only recently come under British rule. The "Non-regulation" provinces "were generally ruled in accordance with simple codes, based on the spirit of the Regulations, but modified to suit the circumstances of each special case." This system on the whole answered well, and in many cases the government of the Non-regulation was sounder than that of the Regulation provinces. The distinction between the two types of provinces has practically disappeared. In matters connected with the administration, however, a few distinctions still survive. In the Non-regulation provinces the executive head of a district is called a "Deputy-Commissioner" and not a Collector, as in the Regulation provinces; and many of the posts reserved in the other provinces for members of the Indian Civil Service are also open to military officers and to others possessing suitable qualifications. This arrangement is now being discontinued in many of the Non-regulation provinces, and in Burma only of the more important provinces are military officers employed very largely as District Officers. In the Non-regulation provinces also the District Officer has larger judicial powers than those in the other provinces.

Madras and Bombay.

The Presidencies of Madras and Bombay are so called because in the early days they were governed by Presidents in Council, and were originally independent of Bengal. In 1839, Aden was captured by the British troops, and is now subject to the Bombay Government. Four years later Sind was conquered by Sir Charles Napier, and after a few years was also merged into the Bombay Presidency. Madras and Bombay are each subject to the rule of a Governor in Council. The Governor is usually a man of high rank and ample experience, who is appointed from England by the Crown, acting on the advice of the Secretary of State. He is assisted by a Council, the members of which are also appointed by the Crown on the advice of the Secretary of State. In 1833, the number of Councillors was three, but was subsequently reduced to two. Until the year 1893, the Commanders-in-Chief of the Madras and Bombay armies were appointed extraordinary members of their respective councils, but this custom ceased with the abolition of these posts, owing to certain changes in the organization of the army. Under the Councils Act of 1909, permission was granted to increase the number to a maximum of four, of whom two at least shall have served in India under the Crown for twelve years or more at the time of their appointment. In both provinces at present the Council consists of three members besides the Governor, two in each case being members of the Indian Civil Service, and the third an Indian gentleman. The Governors of these provinces have the right to communicate direct with the Secretary of State, to override the members of the Executive Council in the same way as the Governor-General, and to issue such regulations for the conduct of work as they may consider necessary, and make certain appointments, which in other provinces are in the hands of the Governor-General, such as Conservators of Forests, and in Madras members of the Board of

Revenue. In both provinces the Members of Council hold portfolios, and are responsible for the general supervision of departments entrusted to their care, matters of importance only being brought before the whole Council.

The administrative history of the Presidency of Bengal requires considerable explanation, and is somewhat complicated. Geographically

Bengal.

the name of Bengal is applied to the deltas of the Ganges and the Brahmaputra, which are inhabited by Bengali-speaking people, but it has politically a far wider scope. Originally, the Bengal administration was confined to the factories and settlements grouped around Calcutta. The neighbouring provinces of Bihar and Orissa were added at the time when the Moghul bestowed the Diwani on the East India Company; and latterly all the British conquests in north-western India have been brought within the same fold. Under the Regulating Act the Governor of Bengal became the Governor-General of Bengal, with certain powers over the other provinces. As time went on, and the boundaries of Bengal were enlarged by successive conquests, the responsibilities of the Governor-General became too great. It was impossible for him to conduct the administration of a large province as well as to control the destinies of British India. In 1833 the partition of Bengal was first mooted. At first it was arranged that there should be a Governor in Council for the new province of Agra, but the appointment was never made. Shortly afterwards, however, Agra was placed under a Lieutenant-Governor. In 1877, Oudh was amalgamated with Agra, and called the North-Western Provinces. As further territory to the north-west was added to the British Dominions in India, the name was changed to that of the United Provinces of Agra and Oudh. After the first Sikh War in 1846, the eastern portion of the Punjab was annexed, and the western part was added three years later. In 1859, the Punjab, together with Delhi and the surrounding country, which were transferred from the North-Western Provinces, was placed under the rule of the Lieutenant-Governor of the Punjab. In very recent years further changes have been made in the boundaries of the Punjab. Certain districts were added to the North-West Frontier Province, which was formed in 1901; and in consequence of the change of capital, Delhi and the surrounding country has been transferred to the direct control of the Government of India.

In the meantime, Bengal itself had been subjected to further changes. In 1853, the Governor-General of India was relieved of all direct responsibility for the administration of Bengal, when a Lieutenant-Governor was appointed for that province. In 1905, further partition being considered necessary, Assam, with a large portion of Bengal, was made into the new province of Eastern Bengal and Assam under the rule of a Lieutenant-Governor. The arrangement was not favourable to the wishes of many inhabitants of the provinces concerned, and in 1911, at the time of the transference of the capital from Calcutta to Delhi, the King-Emperor made a proclamation to the effect that the previous partition should be revised, and a different division of Bengal made. In consequence, Assam became again a Chief Commissionership, a new

Lieutenant-Governorship was formed for Bihar and Orissa, and the remaining portions of the old provinces were placed under the charge of a Governor in Council, who was given privileges and powers similar to those of the Governors of Madras and Bombay.

Lieutenant-Governors.

There were in 1912 four Lieutenant-Governors, being those of the United Provinces, the Punjab, Burma, and Bihar and Orissa. A Lieutenant-Governor is appointed by the Governor-General in Council, subject to the approval of the Crown, and must by statute have served ten years or more in India at the time of appointment. He is almost invariably a member of the Indian Civil Service. The Councils Act of 1909 as first presented to Parliament gave the right to the Governor-General in Council, with the consent of the Secretary of State, to frame regulations for the appointment of Executive Councils for provinces ruled by Lieutenant-Governors. The House of Lords rejected that clause, but after consultation between the leaders of the two parties a compromise was eventually arrived at by which the Governor-General was empowered to create an Executive Council for Bengal, but in the case of the other provinces concerned the draft-regulation appointing the Executive Council should be laid before each House of Parliament for not less than sixty days during the session, and either House could prevent the regulation coming into force by an address presented by a majority of its members. An Executive Council has already been appointed for Bengal under Lord Carmichael, the first Governor. In 1912, arrangements were made for a similar Council in

Bihar and Orissa, and the Government chose to constitute it by means of a special Act of Parliament.

Chief Commissioners.

A Lieutenant-Governorship is constituted under Act of Parliament, and therefore no such province can be formed without reference to Parliament; but this is not the case with territory ruled by a Chief Commissioner, who is appointed by the Governor-General and merely administers territory on behalf of the Governor-General in Council. On the other hand, his executive powers are considerable, and, in many respects, equal to those of a Lieutenant-Governor. In 1861, a Chief Commissioner was appointed for the Central Provinces, and in 1903 Berar, which had been purchased from the Nizam, was added to the territories under his control. As has already been pointed out, Assam is also a Chief Commissionership. The North-West Frontier Province is another, and the Chief Commissioner also assists the Governor-General as Agent in dealings with the frontier tribes. British Baluchistan and Ajmer-Merwara are governed by the Agents to the Governor-General in Baluchistan and Rajputana respectively; and Coorg is administered by the Resident of Mysore. The Superintendent of the Penal Settlement of Port Blair is in charge of the Andaman Isles.

Provincial Secretariats.

Each province, therefore, has its own Local Government. At the headquarters of each are the Government Offices, or, as they are more generally known in India, the Secretariat. The work of the administration is divided among certain departments, over each of which presides a Secretary, who is responsible either to the Member of Council, or, when there is no such officer, to the head of the Government. The Secretaries to Government and the Under-Secretaries are drawn from members of the Indian Civil Service, but the Secretaries to the Public Works Departments are the chief engineers in each province. Each Secretary holds office, as a rule, for a period not exceeding three years, as it is not considered desirable for a civilian to spend all his time at headquarters instead of in the districts, and it is also probable that at the end of such a period he will be promoted to some higher post. In each department there is also an Assistant-Secretary, who is a departmental officer, and does not belong to the Indian Civil Service. Below the Secretaries are the members of the subordinate and clerical staff, who are attached permanently to the Secretariat.

CHAPTER V.

DISTRICT ADMINISTRATION.

"That is the mission with which we have to charge you, and it is as momentous a mission as was ever confided to any great Military Commanders or Admirals of the Fleet. This mission of yours is to place yourself in touch with the people you have to govern."

LORD MORLEY, "Speech to Indian Probationers."

"The principle I adopted for the Civil administration was to preserve unimpaired the practice which I found established."

MOUNTSTUART ELPHINSTONE.

District Officials.

THE backbone of the British Administration in India is the District Officer, known as the Collector in the Regulation and the Deputy-Commissioner in the Non-regulation provinces. A district varies very much in size in different parts of the country, but its average extent is about 5000 square miles, with a population of nearly a million inhabitants. The District Officer is usually a member of the Indian Civil Service, but in the Non-regulation provinces there are still some military and other officers serving in that capacity; and there are a certain number who have been appointed from the Provincial Service to the 'listed' posts.[1] There is good ground for saying that the

[1] See note, p. 22.

whole life of a district corresponds very largely with the strength or weakness of its District Officer. Under the District Officer are Assistant Collectors, who are members of the Indian Civil Service, Deputy Collectors belonging to the Provincial Service, and the subordinate officials, known in some provinces as Tahsildars and in others as Mamlatdars, each of whom has a Taluka, or a group of villages, under his charge. These latter officials have on a small scale much the same duties as the District Officer, to whom they are responsible. They are chosen in some cases by the Commissioners, and in others by the Board of Revenue, and are often men of business capacity and general culture. They are in touch again with the village officials.

The Village Communities.

The Indian village communities have existed from very ancient times, and still play a very prominent part in the social life of the country. In Northern India the villages are usually in the hands of Zemindars or landlords, but in certain other parts of the country the land is tilled by individual owners, though there are certain tracts set apart for grazing in the common interest. Mountstuart Elphinstone, in writing a report on the territories conquered from the Peshwa, has given the following account of the Mahratta village :

" In whatever point of view we examine the Native Government in the Deccan, the first and most important feature is the division into villages and townships. These communities contain in miniature all the material of a State within themselves, and are almost sufficient to protect their members, if all other Governments were withdrawn.

Though probably not compatible with a very good form of Government, they are an excellent remedy for the imperfections of a bad one; they prevent the bad effects of its negligence and weakness; and even present some barrier against its tyranny and rapacity."

Village Officials.

In all villages there are certain officials, whose duties are much the same in all parts of India. The "headman" of the village is called the "Patel," who collects the revenue, and in some provinces is responsible for the maintenance of peace and order. The accountant, who keeps the land records of the village is called the "Patwari" in the north and the "Kulkarni" in the west. Lastly, there is the Chaukidar or watchman, whose duties vary in the different provinces. He is very largely a policeman, who keeps his superior officers informed of the whereabouts and doings of suspicious characters.

Commissioners of Divisions.

Except in Madras, there are in all provinces Commissioners of Division, who hold a position intermediate between the Collectors and the headquarters staff. These officers have no judicial duties, but are concerned chiefly with the collection of revenue and with all questions intimately concerned with the land; and they have supervisory powers in ordinary executive matters over such Collectors as may be in their division. The Commissioner in Sind holds a peculiar position, which has somewhat aptly been described as that of a minor local administration under a major local Government. This means that the Bombay Government has delegated certain of its executive functions to the Commissioner in Sind, who thus holds a stronger position than the other Commissioners in the Presidency.

Though he is the representative of the central administration, and is subject to its orders, the District Officer has to depend in most instances on his own initiative. It is difficult for officers at headquarters to deal with matters requiring a personal knowledge, and the decision is usually left, and rightly, to the District Officer. His duties are manifold. As the title "Collector" suggests, he is the chief revenue officer of the district, and is responsible for the collection of the land revenue and other taxes, and also for the maintenance of land records and registers. He is also a magistrate, and, subject to appeal, is responsible for the effective and prompt administration of criminal justice; and he is in charge of the various departments of public interest. There reside at his headquarters officials of other departments, such as the Superintendent of Police, the Executive Engineer, and the Civil Surgeon; and in certain districts an Inspector of Schools and a Forest Officer. These officials receive orders each from his own superior officer at headquarters, but all matters of importance are laid before the District Officer, who has powers of supervision over all work done in his district. Sir William Hunter has spoken of the duties and responsibilities of the District Officer in the following words:

The District Officer.

"He is a fiscal officer charged with the collection of the revenue from the land and other sources; he is also a Revenue and Criminal Judge both of first instance and in appeal. But his title by no means exhausts his multifarious duties. He does in his small local sphere all that the Home Secretary does in England, and a great deal more, for he is the representative of a paternal and not of a constitutional Government. Police, jails, education, municipalities, roads, sanitation, dispensaries, local taxation, and the imperial revenues of his district are to him matters of daily concern. He is expected to make himself acquainted with every phase of the social life of the natives, and with each natural aspect of the country. He should be a lawyer, an accountant, a financier, and a ready-writer of state papers. He ought also to possess no mean knowledge of agriculture, political economy, and engineering."

Tours.

The District Officer resides for the greater part of the year at his headquarters, but tours round his district during the cold weather. Great importance is attached to the value of these tours. In a country such as India the personal equation enters very largely into the success or failure of the administration. The people have always been accustomed to offer petitions to their rulers, and to acquaint them personally with their needs or any causes of discontent. Those in authority, on the other hand, and especially those belonging to an alien race, need to know the people personally and the conditions of life under which they live. Moreover, the administrative duties are carried out very largely by subordinate officials, whose work needs constant supervision. Accounts have to be examined, and questions asked as to delay or mistakes in the transaction of the ordinary business. Both these objects can be attained by a District Officer or the Assistant Collector during their tours in the cold weather.

More need not be said here of the work of the District Officer, but reference will constantly be made to this subject, and a more detailed account of the various sides of his work will be given in subsequent chapters. The collection of the land revenue will be dealt with in the chapter on Land Revenue; the local administration of justice will form a part of the chapter on the judicature; and the story of education, public works, medical relief and sanitation, and police and jails will be narrated in the chapters devoted to the work of each of these departments. It is only necessary at present to emphasize yet again the importance of the District Officer in the work of the Indian Administration.

There are, finally, certain questions of general interest connected with the District Officer to which some passing reference is necessary.

The District Officer's responsibilities.

The foregoing remarks may lead the reader to think that the District Officer is an irresponsible official, but this is far from being the case. "Lions, but lions under the throne," was the dictum of Bacon with regard to the position of the judges in his time, and this is in some respect true in the case of the District Officer. He has considerable powers, but these powers are limited by the rules laid down by Government for his guidance. He is provided with handbooks, which lay down in the most precise manner possible the conditions under which he is to administer his district. A District Officer has also to submit every year to his superior officer a report dealing with the administration of his district. These reports do not consist merely of a dry statement of facts and statistics, but the District Officer is expected to give his opinion as to the position of things in general, and to make suggestions for any improvements that may seem to him necessary. There is also the Commissioner to be taken into account, through whom correspondence between the District Officer and the Government passes. Public opinion may be voiced directly through the Municipalities or the Local Boards, the nature of which will be explained in the next chapter.

Separation of the Judicial and Executive powers.

It will also be seen that, to some extent, judicial and executive functions are vested in the District Officer, who is responsible for the carrying out of justice, as well as the usual administrative duties. Shortly after the grant of the Diwani, Hastings placed the administration of justice in the hands of the Executive Officer or the Collector, and this system has been maintained, with certain alterations, until the present day. Critics of the Indian Governments emphasize very strongly the need of separating the judicial and executive powers, and insist that justice cannot be administered satisfactorily until this is done. The present system, undoubtedly, is not ideal, but it is maintained that it is the best possible for a country such as India. It should be remembered that the administration of civil justice is in the hands of the judiciary, which is represented in the Districts by the District Judge. In the next place, the Collector is by no means omnipotent as a criminal magistrate, and the District Judge on the one hand, and the High Court on the other have powers of supervision over what is done in the Magistrate's Court; and the duties of the Collector are so manifold that he cannot spend much of his time in the courts. A knowledge of the people and of the customs of the country is an essential for the prompt and efficient administration of justice, and these qualities should be possessed by the District Officer and his subordinates. "The Indian people," said Sir Henry Lawrence, "like all people under the sun, prefer justice to law." There is a great need of speedy and prompt justice, which should be gained in a case tried by the District Officer rather than in one where the lawyer might be involved in petty legal subtleties, wholly unsuitable to the ways of the people. The demands of economy also enter into the question, and the multiplication of officials would make serious inroads on the public purse. Still, the question is difficult, and has received from time to time the most serious consideration of Government.

CHAPTER VI.

MUNICIPALITIES AND LOCAL BOARDS.

"Local assemblies of citizens constitute the strength of nations. Town meetings are to liberty what primary schools are to science; they bring it within the people's reach; they teach men how to use and how to enjoy it. A nation may establish a system of free government, but without the spirit of municipal institutions it cannot have the spirit of liberty."

DE TOCQUEVILLE.

"The cardinal principle, which is essential to the success of self-government in any shape is this, that the jurisdiction of the primary boards must be so limited in area as to ensure both local knowledge and local interest on the part of each of the members."

RESOLUTION OF THE GOVERNOR-GENERAL (LORD RIPON) IN COUNCIL, 1882.

Municipalities of the Presidency towns.

THE introduction of municipal and local self-government into India is of recent origin, and its progress has been slow and fraught with many difficulties and disappointments. A Corporation and a Mayor's Court were established first of all in Madras in 1687, and at a later date in Calcutta and Bombay. At first the functions of the Corporation were very largely judicial, but in the course of time administrative duties were entrusted to its care, and permission was given to raise the necessary taxes within the municipal area. In recent years an elective element has been introduced into the municipalities, but the scope of each varies to some extent. In Calcutta the Municipality used to consist of a nominated chairman and seventy-five councillors, of whom two-thirds were elected. It was found that, though certain improvements had been made, the city was in a very insanitary state, and vast changes were necessary. A new constitution was then drawn up, whereby the councillors were reduced in number to fifty, of whom one-half were elected and the remainder nominated by the Government and other public bodies; and the chairman, who is the chief executive officer, is also nominated by the Government. In Madras only eight of the councillors and the President are nominated by the Government, the remainder being elected either by the ratepayers or by certain public bodies. The Bombay Municipality has had a very prosperous career, and the affairs of the town on the whole have been conducted with business-like moderation and a commendable respect for public responsibilities. There are seventy-two councillors; and of these only sixteen are nominated by the Government, the remainder being elected by the ratepayers, the justices of the peace, the fellows of the University, and the Chamber of Commerce. The President is elected by the councillors, and presides over the meetings of the Council, but the chief executive authority is the Municipal Commissioner, who is a nominee of Government, and at present is a member of the Indian Civil Service.

The responsibilities of these municipalities are very great. Schools, lighting, the water supply, the disposal of sewage, the maintenance of roads, all come under the charge of the Municipality. In the Bombay Municipality there are working under the direction of the Commissioner the permanent Heads of Departments, such as the Executive Engineer, the Water Engineer, the Municipal Secretary, the Superintendents of Markets, Licences, and Gardens, the Curator of the Victoria and Albert Museum, the Chief Officer of the Fire Brigade, and the Storekeeper; and each of these officers administers the affairs of his own department. In addition, the Standing Committee, which is appointed by the Corporation, superintends generally the finances of the Municipality, and there are Committees, such as the Schools Committee and Sub-Committees, appointed for special purposes. The following statement of accounts for the year 1910-1911 will explain how the Municipality raises its income and conducts its expenditure. It is estimated that the average taxation per head of the population of the city amounts to Rs. 10,12,1 peryear.

Bombay Municipality revenue and expenditure.

Net Revenue, after deducting Refunds, Drawbacks, and Charges in respect of assessment and Collection and granting of Refunds.

	Rs.	a.	p.
General Tax - - - -	42,50,171	14	3
Fire Tax - - - - -	34,783	11	0
Wheel Tax and Tolls - -	4,66,316	1	4
Town Duties - - - -	15,54,050	12	7
Receipts from Government for Liquor - - -	4,03,657	6	7
Licences and Tobacco Duty	1,30,384	5	4
Water Revenue (Net) -	3,15,098	13	9
Market Receipts—			
Returns from other Property and Miscellaneous -	4,54,706	8	7
	76,09,169	9	5

Net Expenditure, after deducting Receipts:	Rs.	a.	p.
General Superintendence -	2,52,777	1	10
Fire Brigade - - -	....		
Public Gardens - - -	79,067	13	10
Public Works (including Water Works) - -	18,50,305	0	3
New Works (excluding Water Works) - -	1,52,322	9	3
Public Health Department (excluding Markets) -	5,48,046	13	7
Municipal Debt (excluding Water Works) - -	16,95,295	5	5
Education - - - -	4,17,124	5	5
Hospitals - - - -	4,64,416	5	8
Pensions, Gratuities, Compassionate Allowances	46,298	15	10
Contribution to the City Improvement Trust -	8,35,000	0	0
Miscellaneous - - - -	1,67,003	8	1
Plague Expenses - -	1,87,234	5	11
	66,94,892	5	1
Surplus - - - -	9,14,277	4	4
Rs.	76,09,169	9	5

Loans.

For works involving a large outlay, money is raised usually by loan. In 1910-1911, the total capital debt of the Corporation amounted to Rs. 5,62,88,147. Against this is the sinking fund, which has investments valued at Rs. 1,04,68,215; and the properties of the Municipality, which are valued at Rs. 6,38,80,180. It will be seen, therefore, that the assets exceed the gross liability by a considerable sum, and thus the financial stability of the Municipality is unquestionably assured.

The simplest way to examine the work done by a municipality is not merely to look at the streets, the dwellings, and the people, but to inquire into the death-rate. The answer will quickly show whether the municipality is performing its duties properly in the interests of the town. The following table will show that, though the death-rate in Bombay is still very high, yet the bill of mortality is being considerably reduced. Public Health.

Year.	Number of deaths registered.	Death-rate per thousand.
1896	33,451	40·71
1897	47,896	58·28
1898	51,961	63·23
1899	56,434	68·07
1900	79,350	96·55
1901	59,495	76·66
1902	48,414	62·38
1903	50,513	65·09
1904	42,676	54·99
1905	47,662	61·54
1906	52,874	54·07
1907	38,687	39·56
1908	38,271	39·13
1909	34,878	35·66
1910	34,933	35·72

Before passing to the district municipalities, there are still some matters connected with the life of the Presidency towns which demand attention. At the beginning of the century the population of Calcutta amounted to 809,000, and that of Bombay to 776,000. In the latter city Improvements Trusts.

a large portion of the land now occupied has been reclaimed at one time or another from the sea, and at the present moment large schemes are being considered for further reclamation of what is known as Back Bay; but for all that, the extent of the urban area is necessarily confined, owing to geographical reasons, and in consequence there is much overcrowding. There are in the city large "Chawls" or tenements, each accommodating in some cases up to a thousand people. Some of the streets are narrow and filthy, and fresh air is denied to all but the topmost stories. Mr. Lovat Fraser, who lived many years in India, has stated that "nothing was so terrible as the daily sight of all those vast fetid breeding-houses of death, within earshot of murmuring waves telling of five hundred leagues of wind-swept sunlit ocean." The ravages of plague made those in authority understand the awful squalor and the terrible danger that lurked within that great city. During the rule of Lord Sandhurst the Bombay City Improvement Trust was started, and its policy has been developed within the last few years with very considerable success. The huge tenements are gradually being swept away, and wide avenues carved throughout the length and breadth of the city. Fresh air and sunlight are thus admitted to places which formerly were pregnant with disease and immersed in squalor. The outlying country to the north of the Island of Bombay is being developed, which, with improved means of transit, will soon accommodate thousands of people now living in the city. The Trust was instituted by an Act passed in 1898, and its affairs are administered by a Board of Trustees, of whom the chairman is nominated by the Government, and is at present a member of the Indian Civil Service. Its funds are raised partly by loan and partly by certain vacant Government and Municipal lands, which have been handed over to the trustees; and in 1911 fifty lakhs were given by the Government of India out of their year's surplus. In Calcutta a similar body has been constituted, which is dealing with the congested areas lying chiefly to the north of the city that "skulk behind a fringe of palaces."

Besides the City Improvement Trusts, there are the Port Trusts in the chief sea-port towns.[1] These consist of members nominated either by Government or by the Chambers of Commerce and other institutions interested in the work of the port. In Bombay the chairman of the Port Trust is a member of the Public Works Department. The harbour is being deepened by a system of dredging, whereby the substance can be removed through specially-constructed pipes to places where reclamation works are being taken in hand. By this means two pieces of work of vital importance to the city are being carried out at one and the same time. The money necessary for developing large schemes of improvement is raised

Port Trusts.

[1] The Great Shipping Ports of the British Empire, 1910:

London, - - - -	19,737,350 tons.
Liverpool, - - - -	14,313,514 ,,
Cardiff, - - - -	11,054,916 ,,
Tyne Ports, - - -	10,823,992 ,,
Sydney, - - - -	7,137,308 ,,
Southampton, - - -	6,553,206 ,,
Calcutta, - - - -	6,370,238 ,,
Glasgow, - - - -	5,633,392 ,,
Melbourne, - - - -	5,314,455 ,,
Bombay, - - -	4,195,592 ,,

by loan, and in Bombay a large new dock is being constructed, which will accommodate even the largest steamers which now enter the harbour. With its completion the mail steamers will come straight up to the landing-stage, and much inconvenience will be saved. The Port Trust also administers the port, and renders certain services, such as pilotage, to all ships coming into the harbour, and for these purposes a sufficient revenue is derived from the harbour and the shipping dues that are paid by the ships in question. The revenue of the Calcutta Port Trust in 1910-11 amounted to Rs. 1,18,36,515, and that of Bombay was Rs. 86,93,032 in the same year. The total tonnage of shipping which entered the port of Bombay in 1910-1911 was 4,195,592, and 1,589 vessels were accommodated in the docks during the same year. Similar work is carried out at Karachi, Aden, Madras, Rangoon and Chittagong. Considerable progress has been made by the first-named port, which in future years may equal even the rival harbour of Bombay. It lies in the direct line between Aden and the big centres of population in Northern India, and is comparatively close to those vast tracts of land now rendered fertile by the irrigation policy initiated by the Government of India.

District Municipalities.

We may now turn our attention to the municipalities outside the Presidency towns, which have been springing up within the last few years. In 1909 there were 717 municipalities in India, excluding those of Calcutta, Madras, and Bombay, with a revenue of Rs. 10,50,00,000. More than half of the members of these municipalities are elected, the remainder being nominated by Government. The direct taxation of the people by the municipalities has never been popular in India, and for this reason the early attempts at municipal government were not successful. The present municipal policy dates very largely from the time of Lord Mayo. The objects of this policy are many. It is hoped that the people of the country will be trained thereby in the art of self-government, that the local needs of the city will be better cared for, and that Indians and Europeans will learn to co-operate in the promotion of matters of common interest. Such, undoubtedly, were the views of Lord Ripon, under whose rule great strides were made in the development of municipal life. In some cases the President has ceased to be a Government official, and a Chief Officer has been appointed by the Municipality. The Collector and the Commissioner of the Division have powers of control, and in certain cases Government can suspend a municipality if it thinks that there has been an abuse of powers, and that unsatisfactory provision has been made for the needs of the town.

Work of a Municipality.

The municipal functions are very diverse, and perhaps the Bombay Act of 1901 will explain adequately the everyday work of a Town Council. There are certain duties which are obligatory; and the Act also lays down others which may be undertaken by the municipality under certain conditions. "The following are included in the obligatory list: lighting, watering and cleansing public streets and places; abatement of public nuisances; protection against fire; regulation or abatement of offensive or dangerous trades and practices; removal of obstructions in public streets and places; securing or removing dangerous buildings; reclamation of unhealthy localities; disposal of the dead; construction and maintenance of public streets, culverts, boundary marks, slaughter houses, latrines, drains, sewers, drainage and sewage work, baths, washing places, drinking fountains, tanks, wells, dams, and the like; water supply; naming streets and numbering houses; public vaccination and the supply of animal lymph; public hospitals and dispensaries; primary education; measures of precaution and relief during visitations of epidemic disease, and relief during periods of famine and scarcity." The Act also provides a list of other duties, which the municipalities may undertake under certain conditions and which includes the following: "new streets, public parks, gardens, libraries, museums, halls, offices, rest houses, and other public buildings; education above the primary stage; roadside and other trees; census; records in connection with vital statistics; survey; precautionary measures connected with dogs; places for carrying on offensive trades; sewage arrangements for private premises; sewage farms; public receptions; ceremonies and exhibitions."

To some the rate of taxation, which averages about Rs. 2,2 a head, may appear high; but to those acquainted with the work of the County Councils or municipalities in England it is surprisingly low. For works of great importance money is raised very largely by loan from the Imperial Exchequer, and is subject to the control of Government. The ordinary revenue is raised to some extent from municipal property and grants from the Local Government, but principally by means of taxation. In many of the provinces the Octroi provide the main source of taxation. These are duties levied on articles, principally of food, which are brought into the town for local use; in other provinces there is a tax on houses and lands, and sometimes on professions. There have been instances when the Local Government has found it necessary to intervene on behalf of the general public; but these are rare, and, on the whole, the increased efficiency of the municipalities has been a pleasing feature in recent Indian history.

In the country districts there are Local Boards, to whom are entrusted duties similar to those of the municipalities, but to a smaller degree. The Local Boards, like the municipalities, did not thrive from the very first, but a great stimulus was given during the rule of Lord Ripon. In England, the Local Government in rural areas is placed in the hands of the County, District, and Parish Councils, each possessing certain specific duties. The unit for the purposes of Local Government is the Parish, which is of an ecclesiastical origin. In India the conditions differ in each province which has evolved its own system. In Madras the unit is the village, or a group of villages so constituted that members of the Board have a personal knowledge of all matters brought before them. This village board bears the name of "Panchayat," which originated in the meetings of the old village communities. These public bodies undertake the supervision of sanitary arrangements and other petty duties. Above them are the Taluka Boards, which control matters of general importance. Finally, there are the District Boards, which represent the whole district. Local Government, therefore, is more

Local Boards.

complete in Madras than elsewhere. In the other provinces these three stages are rarely, if ever, found. In the Bombay Presidency there are the District and Taluka Boards.

Constitution and duties of local Boards.

The constitution of these Boards also varies in different parts of the country. The nominated members are more numerous than in the case of the Municipalities, but in many instances the elective element has been introduced and will doubtless be extended from time to time. In 1910-1911 there were on the District and the Taluka Boards in the Bombay Presidency 3645 members; of these 2021 were nominated members and 1624 were elected; and again 773 were officials and 2872 were non-officials. In Bombay and in certain other provinces nomination rests with the Government on the recommendation of the local authorities. The District Officer is the president of the District Board; and a Sub-divisional Officer presides over the Taluka Boards. Besides supervising the maintenance and improvement of the means of local communications the main functions of the District Boards are the maintenance of hospitals and dispensaries; the provision of drainage and water supply; general sanitation; vaccination; education, especially in its elementary stages; the charge of pounds and ferries; the construction and maintenance of markets; and the relief of the population in times of famine. The Sub-divisional or Taluka Boards carry out their duties subject to the supervision of the District Board. The revenues are derived partly from grants made by the Local Governments, partly from a cess on land, and partly from fees for pounds and ferries and other payments derived from road tolls. The accounts of the Local Boards, as well as those of the Municipalities are subject to an audit held by officials of the Government, but are excluded from the Imperial budget.

The following statements of receipts and expenditure of the Local Boards in the Bombay Presidency for the year 1909-1910 will perhaps explain the scope of their work :

Income.	Rupees in thousands.
Land Revenue	1·74
Provincial Rates	32·26
Interest	·16
Receipts from Fees and Charges	3·25
Miscellaneous	·33
Civil Works	4·85
Contributions	25·70
	68·29
Deficit	·90 1/3
	69·19 1/3

Expenditure.	Rupees in thousands.
Administration	1·59
Education	23·77
Medical	3·74
Scientific and other departments	1·24
Stationery and Printing	·18
Miscellaneous	·64
Civil Works	35·47
Contributions	2·01
Debt and Interest	·55 1/3
	69·19 1/3

It will be seen, therefore, that the expenditure is devoted chiefly to education and civil works, the latter consisting of buildings, communications, water supply, tools and plant, staging bungalows, and arboriculture. The medical expenditure includes grants for itinerant vaccinators and the supply of quinine during the malaria season. It appears from statistics that the Local Boards and Municipalities are responsible for 35 per cent. of the total expenditure incurred on roads and buildings in British India, for 43 per cent. of that devoted to medical work and sanitation, and for 47 per cent. of that given to education. The Local Boards, therefore, are taking an ever-increasing share in the administration of the country, and this must be for the good. There is one criticism of a serious nature, that villagers are tending to do nothing for themselves and look to Government or the Local Boards to do everything, such as putting up petty hedges, repairing petty village roads, all of which they used to do in their spare time and at their own cost twenty years ago. It is also reported that in many places the electors are apathetic and indifferent, and that in one district only 79 out of 661 enfranchised electors attended the polls ; and, moreover, that the non-official members, with a few notable exceptions, manifest little interest in the affairs of the Boards, whose success depends mainly on the energy and attention devoted by the District and Taluka Officers.

The development of Local Government has played a great part in English constitutional history. The main feature of Anglo-Saxon times was the strength of the local institutions and the weakness of the Central Government. In Norman times the position was reversed, and increased power was given to the Central Executive at the expense of the local bodies. During the rule of the early Plantagenets a happy compromise was effected, which retained very largely the freedom of the localities to manage their own affairs as well as the efficiency of the Central Government. This was the effect of the evolution of the Parliamentary system which connected the Central Executive with the localities by means of representatives from the counties and big towns The same system, on a small scale, is being effected in India. More and more, as has been seen, the administration of local affairs is being entrusted with the necessary supervision to the District Boards and Municipalities; and the presence of Government officials from the districts and the representatives of Municipalities and District Boards on the Provincial Legislative Councils is bringing the Executive more into touch with local needs and requirements.

Connection between the Local Boards and the Central Government.

CHAPTER VII.

THE LEGISLATURE.

Sovereignty of the British Parliament.

THE British Parliament or—to be more correct—the King-in-Parliament is Sovereign because it has the power "to make or unmake any law[1] whatever; and, further, no person or body is recognised by the law of England as having a right to override or set aside the legislation of Parliament. It can regulate or new-model the succession to the Crown; as was done in the reign of Henry VIII. and William III. It can alter the established religion of the land; as was done in a variety of instances in the reigns of King Henry VIII. and of his three children. It can change and create afresh even the constitution of the kingdom and of parliaments themselves, as was done by the Act of Union, and the several statutes for triennial and septennial elections (and by the Parliament Act of 1911). It can, in short, do everything that is not unnaturally impossible; and therefore some have not scrupled to call its power, by a figure rather too bold, the omnipotence of Parliament."

[1] A law is defined as "any rule which will be enforced by the Courts."

This is not the case with the Indian Legislature, which is what Professor Dicey would call a "Non-Sovereign law-making body." It is Non-Sovereign because it may only make laws subject to the limitations of the Constitution; that is to say, it can only make laws consistent with those passed by the British Parliament having reference to India, such as those referred to in the first chapter; and it has not the right to repeal or to alter any of the Acts of Parliament bearing on the Indian Constitution. Acts of Parliament, however, are not valid in India unless it is stated either by word or by implication that their scope is extended to India. The Indian Legislative Council also cannot repeal or amend the Army Act, nor pass laws affecting the authority of Parliament or any part of the unwritten laws or Constitution of the United Kingdom or the Sovereignty or dominion of the Crown over any part of British India. It must also be remembered that Parliament can at any time pass any law relating to India it pleases, and all Bills introduced by the Government of India must first receive the preliminary approval of the Secretary of State. On the other hand, the Indian Legislature is a law-making body, and can, subject to these restrictions, pass laws (*a*) for all persons, for all courts, and for all places and things within British India; (*b*) for all British subjects of His Majesty and servants of the Government of India within other parts of India; (*c*) for all persons being native Indian subjects of His Majesty or native Indian officers, soldiers, or followers in His Majesty's Indian forces, when respectively in any part of the world, whether within or without His

The Indian Legislature a Non-Sovereign law-making body.

Majesty's dominions; and (*d*) for all persons employed in the Indian Marine Service.

Development of the Imperial Council.

The Legislative Council of India is an expansion of the Executive Council of the Governor-General, its full title being the Governor-General-in-Council at meetings for the purpose of making laws and regulations. Originally, the Company, through the right bestowed on it by charter, could make such regulations or laws as seemed fitting. By the terms of the Regulating Act legislative power was given to the Governor-General-in-Council, subject to the approval and registration of the Supreme Court. Three important steps were taken at the time of the Charter Act of 1833. In the first place, the Madras and Bombay Governments lost their legislative powers, though only for a time, and the legislative authority was vested in the Governor-General-in-Council. Secondly, the Executive Council was enlarged by the addition of the Law Member, whose duties were confined solely to the making of laws and regulations, and who at first did not sit on the Executive Council as a full member; and, thirdly, legislation as passed by this enlarged Council had the full force of law, registration by the Courts being no longer necessary. The principle of extending the Council for legislative purposes was strengthened in 1853 by the inclusion of the Chief Justice of Bengal, a puisne judge, and a member nominated by each of the Local Governments of Bengal, Madras, Bombay and Agra. The Councils Act of 1861 altered the constitution of the Legislative Council still further, and provided that in addition to the members of the Executive Council there should be members not less than six and not more than twelve in number, who were to be nominated by the Governor-General and remain on the Council for two years. Of these extra members, not less than half were to be non-officials; that is to say, men who were not in the service of the Crown. The Head of the Government of the province in which the Council was assembled was an additional member of the Legislative Council. The Act of 1892 increased the number of additional members, and also introduced an elective element by the fact that the non-official members of the recently constituted Legislative Councils of Bengal, Madras, Bombay and the United Provinces and the Calcutta Chamber of Commerce each selected a representative.

Councils Act of 1909.

The Act of 1909 made a bold step further in the same direction. It provided that in addition to the members of the Executive Council there be not more than sixty other members for the purpose of making laws and regulations. Of these not more than thirty-five can be nominated by the Governor-General, who can nominate members in any way he pleases, provided that the majority of all members of the Council be officials, and also that of the nominated members one shall be selected from the Indian commercial community, another from the landholders in the Punjab, and a third from the Muhammadan community in the Punjab. In 1912, the official majority amounted to four. The remaining twenty-five members were elected in the following ways:

(1) The non-official members of the Councils of Madras, Bombay, United Provinces, and Bengal elect two members each, and

those of Burma, the Punjab, and Eastern Bengal and Assam one each - - - - -	11	members
(2) District Councils and Municipal Committees in the Central Provinces - - - - - -	1	"
(3) Landholders in Bengal, Madras, Bombay, United Provinces, Eastern Bengal and Assam, and Central Provinces elect one member each - - -	6	"
(4) The Muhammadan community in Bengal, Madras, Bombay, United Provinces and Eastern Bengal and Assam elect one member each - - -	5	"
(5) The Bengal and Bombay Chambers of Commerce elect one member each - - -	2	"
	25	

A list of rules and regulations with reference to the necessary qualifications of candidates and electors and the manner of election has been issued in accordance with the Act. No person can be eligible for election unless he is a British subject, of sound mind, and over twenty-five years of age. Undischarged bankrupts, men dismissed from Government service, those sentenced by a Criminal Court for a term of imprisonment exceeding six months or debarred from practising as a legal practitioner by a competent authority, are ineligible, but the disqualification in these latter cases may be removed

Rules and Regulations for election.

by the order of the Governor-General-in-Council. Furthermore, the Governor-General-in-Council may debar from election such men as are, in their opinion, of such reputation and antecedents as would be contrary to the public interest. It is also laid down that those elected by the unofficial members of a Provincial Council shall have a place of residence within that province, and have sufficient connection with the affairs of the province as would qualify them to act as its representatives. There are further rules as to the qualifications of voters, lists of which are kept and revised from time to time by the Returning Officers. Precautions are also taken against corrupt practices and for the settlement of disputes arising during the course of the election. It is impossible within the scope of this book to give all the details of these arrangements, but an attempt has been made to show that the Council is representative of the different classes and interests of the community, and that sufficient safeguards have been taken in the interests of minorities. Certain seats are reserved for Muhammadans, and in those Provincial Councils where non-officials return two members a cumulative vote is allowed. By this means a strong minority can give both votes to its candidate and thus secure one of the seats.

Procedure of the Legislative Council.

We may now consider the procedure adopted in the Legislative Council. The President is the Governor-General, who, in accordance with the Councils Act of 1909, appoints the Vice-President to act in his absence. The general arrangements of the Council are in the hands of the Secretary to the Government of India in the Legislative Department or his deputy. It is his duty to keep a journal of the proceedings, which is submitted to the President for his approval after each meeting of the Council. Certain concessions are allowed in the interests of those whose knowledge of English or powers of speech are defective. Bills, reports of select committees, and amendments of important Bills, are translated into Hindustani; any member may speak on behalf of and at the request of another member who is unable to express himself in English; and any member may have his speech printed, a copy of which is given to each member, and at the meeting of the Council the speech may be taken as read at the discretion of the President. To become law a Bill usually goes through the following stages. Any member desirous of introducing a Bill must first of all move for leave to do so. When that is given, the text of the Bill, together with a full statement of its objects, is printed, and a copy is sent to each member. In the case of any contentious measure, the next step is to move that it be referred to a Select Committee, and a debate takes place, during which the general principles of the Bill are considered. The most important stage is then reached, where every detail is discussed, not by the whole Council, but by a Select Committee. A copy of the Committee's report is then sent to each member and also for general publication, and it is afterwards considered by the whole Council, together with any amendments that may be made. Finally a vote is taken, and if it is passed by a majority of votes, it becomes law, subject to the consent of the Governor-General and of the Secretary of State, both of whom have the powers of veto. A non-contentious measure may omit some of these steps and is not referred to a Select Committee. In cases of urgency arrangements can be made so that the Bill may be passed without delay of any kind.

Relations between the Executive and Legislature.

In England the Legislature controls the Executive in that the Cabinet holds office only so long as it has the support of a majority in the House of Commons; but in India the Executive remains in office notwithstanding an adverse vote of the Legislative Council. Sir Courtenay Ilbert has stated that the Legislative Council established under the Act of 1853 modelled its procedure on that of Parliament and showed an inconvenient degree of independence by asking questions and discussing the propriety of measures of the Executive Government. This right to criticize the Executive was revoked by the Act of 1861, which limited the powers of the Legislature to the consideration and passing of laws. These restrictions were slightly relaxed in 1892, when the asking of questions in connection with the administration was allowed under certain conditions, and arrangements were made for the discussion of the annual budget, subject to the proviso, that no member use the privilege to propose any resolution or to divide the Council. The Councils Act of 1909 went very much further in this direction, and Clause 5 reads as follows: " The Governor-General-in-Council shall make rules authorizing at any meeting of the Legislative Council the discussion of the annual financial statement of the Governor-General-in-Council, and of any matter of general public interest, and the asking of questions, under such conditions and restrictions as may be prescribed in the rules."

Discussion of the annual Financial Statement.

It is necessary, first of all, to point out that the financial statement means the preliminary financial estimates of the Governor-General-in-Council for the coming year, and the Budget means the financial statement as finally settled. Every year the financial statement, with an explanatory memorandum, is placed before the Council, and a copy is presented to each member. No discussion whatever takes place on that day. After a short interval the statement is brought before the Council for discussion, and any member may move a resolution relating to any alteration in taxation, any new loan or any additional grant to Local Governments proposed or mentioned in the statement. The Council then proceeds to consider in detail each item or group of items, which are explained by the Member in charge of the department in question; and during this stage resolutions may be moved and a vote taken. After a further interval, during which the Executive has considered the proposals made during the preliminary discussion, and has made such alterations as may be considered necessary, the Budget is laid before the Council. The debate is opened by the Finance Minister, who explains the nature of the changes that may have been made or gives the reasons why the resolutions moved during the earlier stages have not been accepted by the Executive. A general discussion of the Budget then follows and the proceedings terminate. It must be understood that the Budget is in the hands of the Executive and not of the Council. Secondly, any resolution that is moved is only in the nature of a recommendation to the Executive, which may accept it or not as it chooses. Thirdly, the resolutions can only be made under certain conditions. They cannot relate to any of the questions connected with the Indian Constitution or the Army Act, which have been removed from the cognizance of the Council, nor to the relations of the Government of India with any foreign power or any native state in India, nor with any matter that at the time may be under adjudication of any Court of Law in His Majesty's dominions. Such resolutions also may not be connected with the discussion of certain items of revenue and expenditure, such as the Customs, Tribute from Native States, the administration of the Army or Indian Marine, the public debt, or the political department, which subjects are removed from public discussion. And, lastly, the President may disallow any resolution without giving any reason other than that in his opinion it is inconsistent with public interests.

Matters of general interest.

Any member also has the right to move a resolution relative to matters of general public interest. The rules and regulations for such discussions are very similar to those framed for the resolutions moved in connection with the financial statement, but more latitude is allowed and amendments are permitted. The President, however, has the right to refuse discussion on regulations which are inconsistent with public interests, and the resolutions, even if they are passed, are only in the nature of a recommendation to the Executive.

The right of asking questions with regard to the administration that was permitted under certain conditions in 1892 was extended by the Act of 1909, when further or supplementary questions were allowed for the purpose of elucidating any matter of fact regarding which a request for information has been made in the original question. But these questions, both original and supplementary, can only be asked under certain conditions and on certain subjects. They must also be so framed as to be merely a request for information, and not for an expression of opinion. The member who gives the reply may refuse to answer a supplementary question without notice; and the President may disallow any question which, in his opinion, is inconsistent with public interests.

The Right of Interpellation.

The position of the Executive in the Indian Constitution, therefore, is very strong. The control of the purse is in its hands, though, as has been seen, under certain conditions propositions of an advisory nature may be made during the earlier stages of the debate. Criticism of the administration is also allowed with certain restrictions. Any Bill passed by the Legislative Council is subject to the veto of the Governor-General or of the Crown acting through the Secretary of State. The Governor-General also possesses the right in cases of emergency to issue ordinances and proclamations which have the force of law and are recognized by the Courts for six months. This extraordinary power, however, is rarely used.

Position of the Executive.

Provincial Councils.

The history of the Provincial Legislatures is very similar to that of the Imperial. The legislative powers of the Governments of Madras and Bombay were taken away in 1853, when the Imperial Council was remodelled. In 1861, however, legislatures were constituted again in these two provinces, and at later dates in Bengal, the United Provinces, the Punjab, and Burma ; and in 1912 arrangements were made for a Legislative Council for the new province of Bihar and Orissa, and later for the Central Provinces which were still under the rule of a Chief Commissioner. The number of additional members on the various Legislative Councils was increased in 1892, so that there could be a maximum of twenty in Madras and Bombay, and one of fifteen in the United Provinces, and when councils were constituted, in those of Burma and the Punjab. At least one-half of the additional members of Bombay and Madras, and one-third of the other Councils were to be non-officials ; and in Bombay for some years before 1909 there was a non-official majority. The Act of 1909 increased very largely the number of members on the Provincial Councils, and in all cases the official majority has been dispensed with. In the Bombay Council of 1913 the non-official majority amounted to twenty-two. The members are either elected or nominated. The number of elected members also varies in the various provinces, Bengal having twenty-six, Madras nineteen, the Punjab five, and Burma one. In Bombay there are twenty-one, and each has been elected in one of the following ways :

(I.)	Municipality of Bombay - -	1	member.
(II.)	District Municipalities - -	4	,,
(III.)	District Local Boards - -	4	,,
(IV.)	Bombay University - - -	1	,,
(V.)	Bombay Chamber of Commerce -	1	,,
(VI.)	Karachi Chamber of Commerce -	1	,,
(VII).	Indian commercial community -	1	,,

(VIII.) Millowners' Association of Bombay and the Millowners' Association of Ahmedabad alternatively	-	1 member.
(IX.) Muhammadan community -	-	4 „
(X.) Sardars of the Deccan -	-	1 „
(XI.) Sardars of Gujarat - -	-	1 „
(XII.) Jagirdars of Sind - -	-	1 „
		21 „

On all the Councils, except in Burma, there are seats reserved for the Muhammadan community, and in Burma there are nominated non-officials, who represent the Indian, Chinese, and Burmese communities respectively. In Madras, Bombay, Bengal, the Punjab, and the United Provinces the local University elects a member. The landholders, Municipalities, and District Boards also receive representation on most of the Councils. Certain interests are also represented, such as the Planting community in Madras and the Tea and Jute interests in the old Council of Eastern Bengal and Assam. Rules and regulations with regard to the qualifications necessary for candidates and electors and the procedure adopted in the elections have been drawn up. Electoral rolls, which are revised from time to time by the Returning Officer, are published in the Government *Gazette*.

Powers of the Provincial Council.

The powers of the Provincial Councils are fairly extensive. The restrictions placed on the Imperial Legislature and noticed above apply also to the Provincial Councils. The latter also have not the power, except with the consent of the Governor-General, to make or take into consideration any law which affects the public debt or the finances of the Government of India, the currency, post office and telegraphs, the Indian Penal Code, or the discipline and maintenance of His Majesty's naval and military forces. The Local Government also cannot introduce any Bill before the Council without having submitted it first to the Government of India and received its preliminary approval. Every law passed by the local legislature has to receive the assent of the Governor or Lieutenant-Governor of the province concerned, as well as that of the Governor-General; and it may also be disallowed by the Crown, acting through the Secretary of State. The procedure with regard to the proposal of Bills, their reference to Select Committees, and their final acceptance is very similar to that adopted by the Imperial Council and already explained above.

In the Provincial as well as in the Imperial Governments the Legislature is subordinate to the Executive. In Madras and Bombay the Legislative Council is an extension of the Executive for the purpose of making laws and regulations. In Bengal, the Act of 1909 provided for an Executive Council, and thus the basis of the Legislative Council is similar to that in Madras and in Bombay. In the other provinces, as Executive Councils are formed, they will bear the same relation to the Legislature as in the older provinces. In every province where there is a Legislative Council rules have been made regulating the discussion of the annual financial statement of the Local Government concerned, the moving of propositions relative to the public interest, and the asking of questions concerned with the administration. These rules are similar to those in force in the Imperial

Council, subject to the proviso that no proposition will be accepted which deals with such matters as are removed from the cognizance of the Provincial Government.

CHAPTER VIII.

THE JUDICATURE.

"The law itself has been administered without disrespect to creed or caste, or to usages and ideas rooted in your civilisation. It has been simplified in form, and its machinery adjusted to the requirements of ancient communities slowly entering a new world." KING EDWARD VII., PROCLAMATION, 1908.

"In form, intelligibility, and in comprehensiveness, the Indian Codes stand against all competition." SIR HENRY MAINE.

"In the vast field of Indian polity it is in the sphere of law that the English have afforded the highest example of scruple, ingenuity, and tenacity, and it is here that the reader who seeks for practical instruction will find most to learn."

M. CHAILLEY.

"Our first duty, the first duty of any Government, is to keep order." LORD MORLEY.

IN the early days of its rule the Company was satisfied with the provision of Courts for the trial of cases between Europeans, and early in the eighteenth century Mayors Courts were established in the three Presidency towns, with the right of appeal to the Local Government and, in certain cases, to the King-in-Council. At the time of the transference of the Diwani to the Company, Clive set up what was known as the Dual System. Criminal justice remained in the hands of the Nawab and was administered in

The administration of justice in early times.

accordance with Muhammadan law by Muhammadan judges. The collection of the revenues and the administration of Civil justice became subject to the control of the Company's officials, but, as a matter of fact, were still conducted by the old Indian judges. This system soon proved a failure. On being transferred from Madras to Calcutta, Warren Hastings soon showed that organizing ability which was so remarkable throughout his long career in India. The judicial system, amongst others, was revised. In the districts the Collector, a member of the Company's service, was placed in charge of the local Civil Court, where he was assisted by Hindus and Muhammadans; and for petty cases there were subordinate judges. Over and above these were first of all the Provincial Courts of appeal and finally the Sadr Diwani Adalat. Criminal justice was subject to the supervision of the Collector, but was still administered by Muhammadan judges, and a Sadr Nizamat Adalat or final Criminal Court of Appeal was established.

Conflicting jurisdiction.

Shortly afterwards the Regulation Act was passed, which, besides reforming the political government, also dealt with judicial matters. A Supreme Court of Judicature was established at Calcutta, with a Chief Justice and three other judges who were appointed by the Crown. A similar Court was instituted in Madras in 1801 and at Bombay in 1823. Appeal was allowed to the King-in-Council in cases where a sum above Rs. 4000 was involved. The Act, however, was obscure in that it failed to lay down the relations between the Executive and the Courts, or to define the powers of the Supreme Court over the actions committed by servants of the Company in discharge of their official duties. The violent quarrels which took place between the Government and the Supreme Court during Hastings' time caused certain amendments to be made in the Act which strengthened the hands of the former. There was also a vagueness in the Act as to what law should be in force. The Supreme Court administered justice in accordance with the principles and procedure of English law, but the Sadr Courts applied as far as possible Hindu or Muhammadan law in conjunction with such "Regulations" as were laid down from time to time by Government. These Courts, with their conflicting ideas of justice, and their different codes, continued side by side for several years. The administration of justice, therefore, became more and more in a state of hopeless confusion. "In the greater part of India," says Sir John Strachey, "the Criminal Law and Procedure were a jumble, based on the old Mahomedan law eked out and rendered tolerable by the Regulations and Acts of our own Government, by fragments of English law, and by the decisions and instructions of the Supreme Courts." Civil justice was in an even worse state. The same authority is of the opinion that the Civil Courts often seemed to be intended rather for the performance of certain forms and ceremonies than for the administration of justice.

The Civil and Criminal Codes.

The codification of the law, Civil and Criminal, and the rearrangement of the Courts were indicated as essential reforms. Hitherto, as has been seen already, there were two systems existing side by side. For many reasons the British Government had been reluctant to supersede the Hindu or Muhammadan law, and it was one of its guiding principles to respect as far as possible the laws and customs of the country. A compromise whereby the best of both systems, the eastern and the western, could be retained seemed the best solution of the difficulty. It was necessary to examine carefully how much of the old Hindu and Muhammadan law could remain with due regard to the demands of justice and humanity. In 1833 a fourth member of Council was appointed to supervise this work. Lord Macaulay held office for four years, and it is due largely to his efforts that after a lapse of twenty years the Penal and Criminal Codes were completed. Three Commissions, sitting at various times, dealt with the yet more difficult task of compiling a Civil Code. Various writers bear testimony to the excellence of these Codes. "Among all the laws of India," says Sir John Strachey, in connection with the Criminal Procedure Code, "there is none more important than this, which regulates the machinery by which peace and order are maintained, and by which crime is prevented and punished. It describes the constitution of all the Criminal Courts; it defines the power which each Court can exercise; it classifies the offences under the Penal Code or other laws, which each judge or magistrate can try; it regulates the manner in which police investigations are to be carried on; the powers of the police to make arrest, with or without the warrant of the magistrate; the proceedings to be taken for keeping the peace and for preventing unlawful assemblies, and for the removal of public nuisances; the manner in which accused persons are to be brought before a magistrate, in which inquiries or trials are to be held, in which evidence is to be heard and recorded, in which commitments to the Supreme Courts are to be made; it contains rules for the trial of cases with juries and assessors, for the admission of appeals, for the revision of sentences and orders by the Superior Courts, and for many other matters more or less directly connected with criminal procedure." Mr. Chailley also, in speaking of the administration of justice, civil and criminal, in India, states that, "not only judges and pleaders, but officials, high and low, British and native, are thoroughly acquainted with the laws under which they have to work, and understand what these require, permit or forbid." These codes are sometimes revised, the most notable additions being made in 1872 by Sir James Fitz-James Stephen.

The High Courts.

The Indian High Courts Act was passed in 1861, when vital changes were made. The old Courts disappeared, and in their place a High Court was established at Calcutta, Madras, and Bombay; and, a short time later, at Allahabad. In the Punjab and in Rangoon there is a Chief Court, the judges of which are appointed not by the Crown, but by the Governor-General-in Council. In the other Non-regulation provinces the place of a High Court is taken by that of the Judicial Commissioner. There is still a Judicial Commissioner in Oudh and in Sind. Judges of the High Court are appointed by the Crown. Rules and regulations with regard to their salaries and pensions have been drawn up, and may be revised by the Secretary-of-State-in-Council, but no alteration may affect the position of any judge already appointed. Members of the Judicial side of the Indian Civil Service of not less than ten years' standing, and with three years' previous legal experience as a District Judge, barristers of England and Ireland, and members of the Faculty of Advocates in Scotland of not less than five years' standing, and those in India who have had a certain experience as a subordinate judge, or who have practised as a barrister in the High Court for a period of not less than ten years, are all eligible for the bench of the High Court. The Chief Justice must be a barrister with the necessary qualifications, but in the case of a temporary appointment any of the existing judges may be selected. At least one-third of the judges must be members of the Indian Civil Service, and at least another third must be barristers or advocates with the qualifications mentioned above.

Powers of the High Courts.

The High Courts have ordinary original jurisdiction in civil and criminal cases, within such limits of each of the Presidency towns as are laid down from time to time by the Local Government, except at Allahabad, where the High Court has no original jurisdiction beyond the cases of Europeans accused for criminal actions. They are also Courts of Appeal from all the subordinate Courts, Civil and Criminal, within the limits of the province. They are, moreover, the authority in all matters connected with wills, bankruptcy, and in the case of Christian subjects, of divorce. They are not entitled to exercise any original jurisdiction in matters connected with the revenue or its collection, so long as it is made in accordance with the regulations at that time in force. The Governor-General, the Governors, and the members of the Executive Councils are exempted from the jurisdiction of the High Court in any action that any of them may have taken in the performance of his public duties, nor are they liable to arrest or imprisonment. The Chief Justice and the High Court Judges have these same immunities. It is within the province of the Chief Justice to decide what judge or judges shall preside over each case that may be brought before the High Court.

Powers of supervision and rights of appeal.

The High Court also has powers of supervision over all the inferior Courts, and makes rules and regulations, subject to the sanction of the Executive, for the convenient carrying out of business in these Courts. In all cases held in the Inferior Courts the evidence is recorded and submitted when required to the High Court, which is thus enabled to revise, if necessary, the proceedings of these Courts. It has the power to call for returns and demand explanations, and can transfer any suit from one Court to another of equal or superior jurisdiction. A subordinate judge may be suspended by order of the High Court, but the final punishment is in the hands of the Local Government, to whose notice the Court is bound to bring the charges made. An appeal lies from a decision of the High Court in its original capacity to a bench of two or more judges of the High Court. Under certain conditions appeal may be made against the decisions of the High or Chief Courts or of those of the Judicial Commissioners to the Judicial Committee of the Privy Council in London, which may be looked upon as an Imperial Court of Appeal for Indian and Colonial cases.

The administration of criminal justice may

differ to a certain extent in the various provinces, but the main features are the same. There are seven classes of Criminal Courts in most provinces :

Criminal justice.

1. The High Court for cases within the Presidency towns and for appeal from other Courts.
2. The Sessions Court.
3. The Courts of First Class Magistrates.
4. Courts of Presidency Magistrates in the Presidency towns and of City Magistrates in certain other towns.
5. The Courts of Second Class Magistrates.
6. The Courts of Third Class Magistrates.
7. The Courts of Honorary Magistrates of the First, Second, or Third Class.

The relations of these Courts to each other, their constitution, and the procedure adopted in each are subject to the jurisdiction of the Code of Criminal Procedure. In every district there is a Court of Sessions presided over by the Sessions Judge, who may be assisted by Additional or Assistant Sessions Judges. These judges perform much the same duties as a Justice of Assize in England. They try all cases committed to them, and, subject to appeal, may enforce even the maximum penalty, though the death sentence needs the confirmation of the High Court. Below the Sessions Court are those of the Magistrates, which are graded into certain divisions. The Presidency Magistrates, whose Courts are in the Presidency towns, and First Class Magistrates elsewhere, may inflict penalties up to two years' imprisonment, or a fine of one thousand rupees ; and in Non-regulation provinces their powers are even more considerable. Magistrates of the second class may sentence up to six months' imprisonment, or a fine of two hundred rupees, and those of the third class up to one month's imprisonment and a fine of fifty rupees. As a rule, the First Class Magistrates are the Collectors, the Assistant and Deputy Collectors, the second class are the Tahsildars or, in Bombay, the Mamlatdars, and the third class are the head Karkuns. All the magistrates are appointed by the Local Governments and are subordinate to the District Magistrate, whether he be called the Collector or the Deputy Commissioner. Much useful work is done in the big towns by the Honorary Magistrates, who relieve the congestion in the other courts by trying cases of smaller importance. In some parts of India also the Patels possess petty criminal powers, and thus can render prompt punishment for small offences.

Appeal and procedure.

The rights of appeal are more liberal than in England. An appeal may be made against the decision of a second or third class magistrate to the District Magistrate, or to any other first class magistrate specially empowered; and appeals from the decisions of a first class magistrate may be made to the Sessions Judge, whose original decisions are subject to appeal to the High Court. In any instance where there may appear to have been some irregularity in any of the Lower Courts the High Court has the right to call for papers, make investigations, and, if need be, reverse the decision of the Lower Court. The prerogative of mercy can be exercised in India either by the Governor-General or by the Local Government concerned. In India, criminal cases are sometimes tried by a jury, but the system is somewhat different from that practised in England. In the High Court the jury consists of nine persons, and in other places of such number up to nine being uneven as is decided by the Local Government. It is not necessary in India, as in England, for the jury to be unanimous. Many complaints are heard as to the inefficiency of the jury system, and, undoubtedly, in many countries it is very difficult to find a satisfactory jury. This has been the case sometimes in India, and in many districts juries have not been appointed; and in lieu of them there are assessors who help, but do not bind, the judge by their opinion. Moreover, in the event of a verdict of a jury appearing to be radically wrong the Sessions Judge may refer the case to the High Court for revision. There is one exception to the rule that all criminal cases before the High Court are tried by a jury. The Criminal Law Amendment Act of 1908 provides a special procedure in the case of those tried for offences committed against the State. In these instances the case may be decided by a bench of three judges, but the sanction of the Governor-General-in-Council or the Local Government must first of all be obtained. The duty of holding an inquest on the dead bodies of those who have come to an untimely end are performed in India by the police, subject to the orders of the magistrate; but in Calcutta and Bombay there is a Coroner who is assisted by a jury.

Civil Justice.

In Civil as well as in Criminal Courts there are slight differences in the arrangements and the names of Courts in the various provinces. Roughly speaking, the Civil Courts may be divided into these classes :

1. The High Court.
2. District Courts.
3. Small Causes Courts.
4. Courts of First Class Subordinate Judges.
5. Courts of Second Class Subordinate Judges.

Within the limits of the Presidency towns all civil cases would ordinarily come before the High Court, but for a speedy and a less expensive system of justice Small Causes Courts have been established. These Courts, subject to certain conditions, deal with money suits, where the amount involved does not exceed two thousand rupees, and, in certain cases, where both parties agree, suits involving a sum over and above two thousand rupees can be tried there. They may be likened to the County Courts in England, and both have served a very useful purpose in hastening the wheels of justice and lessening the cost of litigation. There is no appeal from the Small Causes Court, though in certain cases the judge can refer to a higher Court. In the districts there are similar Courts established, but the limit of cases which may be tried in them is lower than in those of the big towns.

The District Judge.

The District and Sessions Judge, besides his duties as a criminal judge, already described, is responsible for the management of all the inferior Civil Courts within his district, and it is his duty to distribute the work amongst those Courts. Every suit is tried in the lowest Court competent to try it. The subordinate judges are divided into certain fixed classes, and may try cases up to the amount permitted in their class. In some of the provinces there are village munsifs who may try cases of a petty nature, and, subject to the agreement of both parties, matters of a greater importance may be brought before them. There is a right of appeal against decisions of the subordinate judges to the District Court, and, in some instances where a large sum of money is involved, to the High Court direct, whilst appeals may be made to the High Court against the original decisions of the District Court, and, on points of law, against its judgments on appeal.

European Subjects and the Courts.

A very large number of the judicial posts are in the hands of the Indians themselves. It has been seen already that Indians may, and often do, sit on the bench of the High Court. The District and Sessions Judges are usually recruited from the members of the Indian Civil Service,[1] but almost all the posts inferior to that of a District or Assistant Judge are filled by Indians. A few words are necessary as to the position of European British subjects in Indian Courts. In civil cases no distinction whatever is made between Europeans and non-Europeans. Till comparatively recent times European subjects could only be tried for criminal offences before a High Court, and, in consequence, much injustice was done to Indians who were forced to prosecute in an expensive Court perhaps hundreds of miles away. In 1872 the rule was relaxed, when magistrates of the highest class and Sessions Judges were allowed to try criminal cases where Europeans were involved, and to inflict punishment within certain limits. In 1883, what is known as the Ilbert Controversy took place. The Government of India proposed largely to extend the jurisdiction of the Inferior Courts over Europeans,

[1] See note on p. 22.

but this proposal met with the keenest opposition from certain quarters. Eventually a compromise was arrived at. Europeans may now be tried before an Indian magistrate or judge who has attained the rank of a District Magistrate or a Sessions Judge respectively, but he retains the privilege of claiming to be tried by jury, one half of which must be composed of Europeans or Americans.

Law Officers.

Reference has already been made to the Law Member of the Governor-General's Council and to the duties he has to perform. In the services of the Provincial Governments is the Legal Remembrancer, whose duty is to draft the Bills submitted to the Legislative Council, and to advise Government generally on legal matters, and he, or his assistant, acts as Secretary to the Legislative Council. In some provinces there is an Advocate-General, who is a member of the Legislative Council, and advises Government as to the conduct of its cases. A similar agency is utilized in the lower grades of the judicature. In the District Courts the officials are assisted by Government pleaders, who conduct cases on their behalf before the Courts. In the Presidency towns there is a sheriff. He is appointed by Government for a period of one year, and is a citizen of high standing. His judicial duties consist mainly in the empanelling of juries. In his public capacity he may be called upon to summon public meetings for the discussion of matters of great importance.

CHAPTER IX

THE POLICE AND JAILS.

Difficulties of Police in India.

THE financial statement on page 122 shows that a large annual grant is given to police and jails; and the amount is steadily rising. In the first year of the century, roughly speaking, £3,000,000 was spent on these purposes, but in 1910-11 the amount was £4,700,000. The maintenance of law and order in a country such as India, where the population is so scattered, must necessarily be both important and expensive; and the combination of efficiency and economy is a task of the greatest difficulty. In the early part of last century Lord Hastings was engaged in warfare with the Pindarees, an outlaw tribe, when a force of over a hundred thousand men had to be employed before the enemy were defeated. Some time later there were bands of men, known as Thugs, bound to each other by ties of secrecy and co-operation, who infested the country and robbed the unwary traveller. Owing to the devoted zeal of Lord William Bentinck, Sir William Sleeman, and others, these horrible crimes were put down, but there is still much to be done. Robbery is very easy in India, where houses cannot be closed at night as in cooler climates, where the people are accustomed to carry their wealth on their persons in the shape of jewellery, and where wholesale brigandage, known as dacoity, is still practised.

Organization of the Indian Police.

In the days of the Company there was very little attempt made at any organization of a public system of police. In 1861, however, a commission of inquiry was held and proposals were made for the provision of a police force. There can be little doubt that in recent years there has been a vast improvement in the organization, honesty, and efficiency of the police. A commission of inquiry was appointed in 1902, which issued a report of much importance and suggested improvements which would increase the annual cost of the police by a sum of £1,000,000. The management of the police is in the hands of the Provincial Governments, each of which has its own constabulary; and, indeed, in Bombay each district has its own force. At the head of each provincial department is an Inspector-General, who is assisted by his deputies located in various parts of the province. In each district there is a District Superintendent of Police, who is assisted by Assistant and Deputy Superintendents. The highest or imperial branch of the police service is recruited by means of a competitive examination in England. The deputy superintendents are usually appointed locally, and may on promotion hold posts usually filled by members of the imperial service. In the Bombay Presidency there is the Central Police Training School at Nasik, where the young officers, whether they be appointed locally or from England, are given a training in law, languages and in drill. In the

Presidency towns and in Rangoon there is a separate organization under the charge of a special commissioner, who is sometimes a member of the Indian Civil Service. There is also a separate force for the protection of railway property, under the command of a railway officer. In addition to the ordinary police, there is a reserve which may serve useful purposes. Recruits are taught their duties during a term of service in the reserve; escorts are provided, and a force is ready at hand to go to any district where help may be required. There is also the Central Criminal Investigation Department—originally the Thagi and Dakaiti Department—whose duties are to collect information and, if possible, to bring to justice gangs of men who commit offences in various parts of the country, and thus baffle the efforts of the local police.

The Village Police.

The ancient village communities in India, as well as in England, were held responsible for the maintenance of law and order, and for the suppression of crime. Mountstuart Elphinstone has given the following description of the duties of the village police in the Deccan during the rule of the Mahrattas. "The Patel is responsible for the police of his village, and is aided, when the occasion requires it, by all the inhabitants. His great and responsible assistant in matters of police is the village watchman (Chaukidar). Though there is only an allowance for one watchman in a village, the family has generally branched out into several numbers, who relieve and aid each other in their duties. The duties are to keep watch at night, to find out all arrivals and departures, observe all strangers, and report all suspicious persons to the

Patel. The watchman is likewise bound to know the character of each man in the village, and in the event of a theft committed within the village bounds, it is his business to detect the thief." The system does not appear very satisfactory, but Elphinstone found the country by no means a scene of anarchy and disorder, and he contrasted the state of the Deccan very favourably with that existing in Bengal at the same time. This satisfactory state of affairs may, in his opinion, have been due to some extent to the fact that all the powers of the State had been united in the same hands, and also that trial was summary and punishment prompt and severe.

Village Police under British Rule.

It has been the policy of the British Government in India, as far as possible, to adapt its methods to the habits and customs of the people. Elphinstone tried to preserve unimpaired the system he found in operation and was content mainly with a closer supervision over the village police. The commission of 1861 also advised that the old village police be retained on their existing footing. In Madras the village headman is responsible for the maintenance of law and order; and in the bigger villages of the Bombay Presidency there are, besides the Patels, the Police Patels, who have petty criminal powers; in certain other parts of India, as in Sind, the zemindars assist Government in the preservation of law and order. The Chaukidar also remains, and his duty is to report crime; but his functions are various, and extend to the arrest of offenders, the general aid of the police, the maintenance of watch and ward over bad characters and suspicious persons, and the general supply of local information.

He receives rent-free lands or small sums of money from Government.

Responsibility of the People in maintaining Law and Order.

A police system, however efficient it may be, cannot be really satisfactory, unless it is supported by the people themselves. Great efforts are being made to render the police efficient. In olden times people, both in England and India, were held responsible for keeping the peace. A citizen was bound not merely to abstain from criminal actions himself, but also to assist in bringing offenders to justice; he was indeed his "brother's keeper." The old system, dependent entirely on the village organization, is obviously out of date to-day, but the present system needs for its success the active support rather than the passive opposition of the people for whose benefit the force is maintained.

Methods of Punishment.

The imposition of punishments and the maintenance of jails is a difficult problem in any country. In England, up till almost recent times, the Penal Code was very severe and the punishment of death was meted out for what would now be considered petty offences. The result was that those who had committed small thefts were tempted to murder their victim and thus render escape more secure, the punishment in either case being the same. The number of serious crimes, therefore, was increased to a most alarming extent. Under Muhammadan rule in India we read that impalement, mutilation, and flogging were ordinary forms of punishment; and in the early date of the British occupation mutilation was still practised. Vast improvements in these respects have been made both in England and in

India during recent years. The limit of punishment for each offence has been laid down in the Indian Penal Code, and the more serious offences can only be tried before the highest tribunals. Changes have also been made by the advance of modern civilization in the methods adopted in judging the heinousness of an offence. In the olden days it was the amount of damage done which constituted the crime, and the punishment varied accordingly. Modern justice seeks rather to find out the motives which inspired the crime. The cold-blooded murder of a poor man is far more worthy of severe punishment than the murder of a rich man for reasons of self-defence or under extreme provocation.

Prisons in olden days.

The condition of prisons in the olden days was also very bad in England as well as in India. The prisoners were herded together in overcrowded and insanitary jails, hardened offenders and comparatively innocent boys inhabiting the same wards. Under such depressing circumstances the latter soon learnt to imitate the former, and left the jail without hope. The prisons and even the courts were death-traps of disease, and there was in many cases little chance of the prisoner leaving the jail alive. Moreover, punishment was meted out with extraordinary severity and brutality.

Improvements in the Prison System.

It was towards the end of the eighteenth century that a feeling of dissatisfaction arose. John Howard took the matter in hand, and within a few years visited almost every jail in England. In consequence of his action many changes were instituted, and to-day the English prison is a very different place from what it was a hundred years ago. A prison is now not merely a place of punishment, which is necessary, if only as a deterrent to others, but also one where the character of the delinquent may be improved by steady discipline and by learning a trade which he can practise after his release. In Indian prisons also reforms have been made. Sir John Strachey is a keen supporter of the present system. "Every district," says he, "has its jails, and there are central prisons in convenient situations. Although not in all respects managed on the system adopted in England, there are few countries in Europe where the jails are so well looked after. A great Indian prison is a model of cleanliness and good management."

Organization of the Prison Service.

In each province there is an Inspector-General of Prisons who is usually a member of the Indian Medical Service, as also as a rule are the superintendents of the central jails. The district jails are subject to the inspection of the District Officer and the Civil Surgeon. The jailors are members of a specially graded service, and in some cases certain convicts are employed to supervise the others. Besides the central and district jails there is the penal settlement at Port Blair in the Andaman Isles, whither those sentenced to transportation are sent. Provided that his conduct has been satisfactory, a convict can, after a certain number of years, settle down on a plot of land and send for his family; and indeed most of the convicts are employed in some sort of work. The whole settlement is in charge of the superintendent, who is responsible to the Government of India. In India itself, the central prisons are reserved for those sentenced to a long term of imprisonment, whilst the district and local jails are used for those convicted of minor offences.

A few features of the present system may now be added to indicate the lines of improvement. Much importance is attached to discipline. The average length of a day's work amounts to nine hours. In some cases the convicts are employed on large public works outside the walls, but they are usually confined within the prison compound. The ordinary work of the jail is done by them, and, besides, they engage in such business as tent-making, printing, and carpet manufacture. By such means the expenses of the establishment are reduced, and, what is far more important, the prisoners learn habits of industry, which, it is hoped, are retained after their release. The various classes of criminals, the women, the sick, and the habitual offenders, are kept separate as far as possible.

Improvements in the Indian Jails.

Boy offenders are sent to Reformatory Schools. In the Bombay Presidency there is such an institution at Yeravda, near Poona. The discipline is naturally stricter than in the ordinary school, and instruction is given not only in reading and writing, but also in industrial work. Some of the boys are engaged in carpentry and others in blacksmith's work, or in painting, polishing, and book-binding. An attempt is made not only to give the boys a new start in life, but also to keep in touch with them after they have left the school. Great progress has also been made in the improvement of the sanitary arrangements of

Yeravda Reformatory School.

the prisons, by which the death-rate has been decreased, and at the present time is very little higher than that of the working classes outside. The death-rate of prisoners in Bombay in 1910 was the lowest on record for the Presidency.

CHAPTER X.

FINANCE.

"The essence of Indian finance lies in the relations between the Imperial and the Provincial Governments. The Imperial Government has to finance itself, but it has also to see that the Provincial Governments are not starved."

The Times (Leading Article).

Control over the Indian Finances.

THE Act of 1858 laid down that the expenditure of the revenues of India, both in India and elsewhere, shall be subject to the control of the Secretary-of-State-in-Council, and no grant or appropriation of any part of such revenues shall be made without the concurrence of a majority of votes at a meeting of the Council. Since that time, the spending powers of the Governor-General-in-Council, and of the provincial Governments have been extended very largely, but the financial control vested in the Secretary of State is still very considerable. Strict rules are laid down to prevent the Government of India from incurring fresh expenditure and increasing the number of its officers above certain limits. The British Parliament has no control over the Indian revenues, except that no money can be spent on military operations beyond the frontier and no additions can be made to the public debt without its consent. A financial statement is placed before the House of Commons every year, but a proposition only that such accounts are in order is put to the vote. Great Britain contributes nothing directly towards the maintenance of the Indian Empire. The cost of the British army garrisoned in India, the salary of the Secretary of State, and the expenses of his establishment are paid from the Indian revenues. Indirectly, however, India gains much from her connection with Great Britain in the protection of her fleet, towards which she contributes about £100,000 a year, and in the low rate of interest she pays on such money as she chooses to borrow.

Characteristics of good Finance.

In the management of the finances of any country these points should especially be noted: (1) The collection of the taxes should be made in the most economical and business-like manner possible. In some countries the cost of collection has been so great that by the time the proceeds of the tax reach the Exchequer very little remains. In other cases, either through the weakness of the administration, or through the fact that certain people are exempt from payment, the tax is not levied to its fullest extent; or, again, the system of "farming" the taxes is in vogue. In these instances, the privilege of collecting the tax is sold to an individual or individuals, who keep for themselves whatever they may collect over and above the amount paid to the State for the privilege. This is a particularly iniquitous system in that it is uneconomical and may also lead to the oppression of the poor. (2) The taxes should be of such a nature that they provide the State with an amount sufficient for the needs of the administration, and their burden should fall on all sections of the community, and especially on those most capable of paying. (3) The expenditure should be carried out without unnecessary extravagance.

Management of Indian Taxation.

Let us now see how far the management of Indian finances is conducted satisfactorily in these respects; and also to what extent the changes made in recent years have improved the system. In the old days of Company rule there was no definite finance department to supervise the collection and expenditure of revenues. After the Government was transferred to the Crown, Mr. James Wilson came out to India as the first finance member. The problems that awaited his decision were very difficult. Owing to the Mutiny the debt of the country had been increased very considerably, and there was need of increased expenditure in almost every department to enable the Government of the country to be carried on and order to be restored. Certain new taxes were levied, but it was chiefly by careful management that the position was improved.

Provincial Governments and Finance.

The second stage in the history of Indian finance is now reached. It is essential that those who spend the money should also have some responsibility for its collection. This used not to be the case in India. At first, the Government of India kept all financial control in its own hands, and the provincial Governments had little incentive to economy. Sir John Strachey in this connection has written these words: "The result was a complete absence of real financial control, frequent wrangling between the supreme and provincial Governments, and interference by the former, not only in financial but in administrative details, with which the local authorities alone were competent to deal." His brother, Sir Richard Strachey, has added that "the distribution of the public income degenerated into something like a scramble, in which the most violent had the advantage, with very little attention to reason; as local economy brought no local advantage, the stimulus to avoid waste was reduced to a minimum, and as no local growth of the income led to local means of improvement, the interest in developing the public revenues was also brought down to the lowest level." In 1867, Lord Mayo saw that some financial responsibility had to be delegated to the Local Governments. At first a fixed sum was given to each, and thus increased expenditure could be met either by more careful management or by local taxation. Some ten years later, Lord Lytton, acting on the advice of Sir John Strachey, substituted a share in the revenues for the fixed grant. By these means the Local Governments were interested not merely in economical expenditure, but also in the careful collection of the revenues. The amount of the share was at first subject to revision, but during the early years of this century a more permanent arrangement has been made. As will be seen later, there is a division of items between the Central and Local Governments under the headings, imperial, provincial, and divided. The revenues are divided up, roughly speaking, as follows: salt, opium, customs, and tribute from native states are wholly imperial. Land revenue, stamps, excise, and assessed taxes are divided between the Central and the Local Governments; and the provincial Governments take all receipts under registration. It is calculated that the Local Governments between them receive rather more than a third of the Indian revenues. The expenditure is divided up along these lines. Home charges, payment of interest on debt, the maintenance of the defence forces, the central administration, and foreign affairs are wholly imperial. Certain departments, such as the post office and telegraphs, the mint, and the railways, have a general rather than a purely local interest, and are therefore also imperial. Irrigation is divided between the two accounts. Local Governments supervise the expenditure on such matters as education, police, health and sanitation. They have therefore large powers and considerable responsibilities, but they are merely the delegates of the supreme Government, and exercise financial and other functions subject to its approval and control. Moreover, they have no borrowing powers, and their budgets have to be submitted beforehand to the Government of India for sanction. All accounts are audited by the officers of the accounts and audit department, who are responsible to the Government of India. In each province there is an Accountant-General, whose "duty is to bring to notice all cases in which a spending authority has exceeded its powers, and to require that such expenditure be disallowed, if not sanctioned by the authority which is competent to pass it." There is also the Comptroller and Auditor-General, who supervises the work of the provincial Accountants-General, and compiles the finance and revenue accounts which are annually submitted to Parliament. The Decentralization Commission recommended that the financial powers of the provincial Governments be increased. The work of supervision has also, to some extent, been handed over to the select committees of the Legislative Councils, which may make suggestions, and also to the members of the various Councils, who may submit resolutions and criticise generally or in detail the financial proposals of the Government. The provincial accounts are included in those of the Government of India, but those of the municipalities and local boards remain separate; as will be remembered, much of the work of education, sanitation, and public works is performed by these bodies.

Revenues of India.

The revenues of India are derived from various sources. As has been noticed already, some are collected by the Imperial and others by the Local Governments. For purposes of classification they may be divided under these headings: Land Revenue, Revenues derived from taxation, Revenues derived from sources other than taxation. The figures given below are those for 1910-11 which were presented in a report to the House of Commons. They are made out, therefore, in English coinage and not in rupees. They represent the *net* income and the *net* expenditure, but the cost of collection is included. It will be seen that, roughly speaking, 36 per cent. of the revenues come from the land, 20 per cent. from commercial undertakings, such as the post office and the railways, and 44 per cent. only from taxation. It is estimated that the average payment of taxation by each person amounts to Rs. 1/5; and, if Land Revenue be included, to Rs. 2/9½.

Net Income, 1910-11.

Land Revenue - - - - -		£20,112,161
Revenues from sources other than Taxation—		
Forests - - -	£1,822,988	
Tribute from Native States - -	408,694	
Opium - - -	6,271,531	
Railways - - -	2,017,496	
Irrigation - -	584,387	
Post Office - -	46,030	
Telegraphs - -	20,327	
Mint - - -	103,741	
		11,275,194
Revenues derived from Taxation—		
Salt - - -	£2,919,767	
Stamps - - -	4,757,510	
Excise - - -	6,957,379	
Provincial Rates -	552,860	
Customs - - -	6,497,001	
Assessed Taxes -	1,583,683	
Registration - -	424,645	
		23,689,845
Exchange - - - - -		70,084
		£55,147,284

Land Revenue is such an important and complicated subject that it will be considered apart from the other sources of revenue in the next chapter.

I. *Revenues derived from Taxation.*

(a) *Salt Tax.* The history of the salt tax in India is interesting to all students of public finance.

It is the only tax which must be paid even by the poorest classes. A tax on salt is enforced in France, Germany, and other countries of Europe. In India, the revenue is derived partly from a tax on imported salt and partly by an excise duty on salt manufactured in the country, either by licensed factories or by a Government monopoly. Thirty years ago the amount of the duty was different in the various provinces, and this gave rise to the levying of customs duties on salt taken from one province to another. This was a very costly arrangement, and, moreover, it became a great hindrance to trade of all kinds. In 1882, the Government of India very wisely made arrangements for an equalization of salt duties in all the provinces. The amount of the duty has also varied. In 1888, the rate was raised from Rs. 2 to Rs. 2-8 a maund, but in 1903 it was reduced again to Rs. 2, and in 1907 to one rupee. This was a wise measure. The amount raised by the tax has decreased a little, but not to such an extent as would be expected, as owing to the cheapness of salt much more is consumed. The fluctuations in the amounts raised by this tax are interesting, as they provide a sure index to the prosperity or depression in the country. In good times much salt is purchased; in times of famine very much less is consumed. The Salt Department in the Bombay Presidency is controlled by the Commissioner of Salt, Excise, etc., who is assisted by a Collector, Assistant Collectors and minor officials.

(b) *Stamps*. This revenue is derived from two sources. In India, as in other countries, stamps must be placed on commercial documents. Besides these, fees are levied by the same means on proceedings in the law courts. The latter can scarcely be considered a tax; it is rather a payment or a contribution towards the maintenance of the courts by those who avail themselves of its services.

(c) *Excise or Abkari.* This item of revenue is raised from licences, fees, and duties levied on the sale of intoxicating liquors and drugs. Originally the system of "farming," as already explained, was in force, and the privilege of manufacturing and selling these articles was sold to private persons. This arrangement has been modified of late years. The control of the excise is very largely in the hands of Local Governments, and each has its own system. Imported liquors come under the heading of "Customs," but the sale of licences to hotels, restaurants, and places of amusement is included in "Excise." The Commissioner of Salt, Excise, etc., in the Bombay Presidency proper and the Commissioner in Sind in that province are in charge of the administration of this department in that Presidency.

(d) *Customs.* The history of this tax has also been interesting and subjected to much criticism from time to time. The State has to consider not merely the collection of revenue, but also how far the imposition or remission of duties will affect the trade of the country.

It is not within the scope of this book to deal with the merits or demerits of a protective system, but it may be pointed out that both in England and in India opinions on this question are very varied. In 1860, imports were taxed at the rate of ten per cent. and in some cases an even higher duty was levied. In subsequent years the duty was reduced, and in 1875 it stood at five per cent. Proposals originating from the Home Government were then made to abolish the tax almost entirely, and were met by strenuous opposition from India. The Viceroy, Lord Northbrook, resigned rather than abolish the duties, and Lord Lytton succeeded him. The new Viceroy, by the help of his Finance Member, Sir John Strachey, was able to make a start in the new policy by reducing the cotton duties, although he had to overrule the majority on his Council. The total abolition of the import duties followed, except those on salt and liquor, which were retained to counterbalance the excise duties levied within the country on these articles. In 1894, the poverty of the Exchequer demanded an increase of taxation. In consequence, an import duty of 5 per cent. was imposed, but an exception was made in favour of cotton. After some further changes, a duty of 3½ per cent. on cotton goods was levied, as well as an excise duty of an equal amount on all cotton manufactured in Indian mills. It was hoped at the time that the arrangement would prove an encouragement to the hand-loom industry of the country, but how far it has been successful is open to question. In 1912, this import duty of 3½ per cent. on cotton and one of 5 per cent. on other goods were still in force, with certain exceptions. Exemption from duty is allowed in the case of certain imports, such as railway materials, machinery, books, coal, and other articles, and a reduced duty of 1 per cent. only is levied on iron and steel. On the other hand, the duty on petroleum, silver bullion, tobacco, and alcoholic drinks have been very largely increased. For the purpose of carrying out this work a Customs Service has been constituted, which is administered by officers recruited either in England or India and a Subordinate Staff.

In 1860, there was an almost general export duty of 3 per cent. These duties have all been remitted, except that on rice, where a duty of three annas per maund is imposed. There is also a small export duty on tea, but the money raised in this instance is used definitely for the encouragement of the Indian tea industry.

(e) *The Income Tax* was first of all imposed in 1860. Since then it has been abolished and restored; and it is still in force. It is not imposed on incomes derived from agriculture or the tenure of land, or upon those of any kind which are less than Rs. 1000 a year. Moreover, it is graduated in such a way that the rich pay on a higher scale than those who are only moderately well off, the poor being exempt altogether. The rate is at 5 pies in the rupee on incomes of Rs. 2000 and over, at 4 pies in the rupee on those between Rs. 1000 and Rs. 2000. Soldiers whose incomes are less than Rs. 500 a month, and all charities and religious endowments, are exempt. The imposition of the income tax has caused much discontent in the past, but it is manifestly a fair means of taxation. It falls on the shoulders of the rich, and of many who otherwise would scarcely be paying their fair share of taxation. It is also the only direct tax imposed in India, and as such induces those who contribute to be more favourable to economy, and opposed to extravagant demands on the public purse.

(f) *Registration.* This item usually is very small.

It is necessary for all deeds of mortgage on the transfer of immovable property to be registered, for which certain fees, the amount of which depends on the value of the property, are charged.

II. *Revenues derived from sources other than taxation.*

(a) *Opium.* "In British India the Government prescribes rules for the cultivation of the poppy, the manufacture, possessions, transport, import or export and sale of opium, and any contravention of such rules is subject to stringent penalties, which may extend to imprisonment for one year, a fine of 1000 rupees, or both." Opium is also produced in certain native States, and is known as Malwa opium ; and on this a very heavy export duty is paid. There has been in the past a very considerable export of opium to China, the proceeds of which have brought in a large income to the Indian Government. In 1906, the Chinese authorities, being aware of the baneful results arising from the large consumption of opium by the Chinese, asked the British Government for its assistance in suppressing its use. The Government of China stated its intention of checking the cultivation of the poppy within its dominions, and asked that the import of opium from India should also cease. It was arranged, therefore, that the Indian opium exports should decrease in amount by one-tenth every year until its final extinction in the year 1919. This is now being done, and it is anticipated that this source of income will cease within a few years.

(b) *Forests.* Of late years the Indian Government have considered it one of their chief duties to look after afforestation. The careful supervision of forests affords not merely an annual income from the sale of timber, but also helps to bring about an increased rainfall. The work of the Forest Department will be referred to in a later chapter.

(c) *Posts and Telegraphs.* Of late years Government has usually gained a small profit on these items, which is the most satisfactory position possible. Its object is not to raise a revenue on this account, but to regulate the postal and telegraphic services on behalf of the people at the cheapest possible rate. In no country in the world are letters carried at so cheap a rate as in India. The business undertaken by these departments has increased very largely in recent years. In 1856, 38,000,000 letters, newspapers, or parcels were delivered, but in 1911-12 the number had risen to 950,000,000. The profits are used very often for the improvement of the services.

(d) *Railways and Irrigation.* The policy of the Government of India with regard to the control and management of the railways and irrigation works will be dealt with later. Most of the railways in India are the property of the State. Till the beginning of the century they were run at a considerable loss to the Government, but since that time, with one exception, the railway budget has shown a balance of receipts over expenditure, which includes working costs, the payment of interest on all loans, and all other charges.

(e) *Tribute from Native States* is a small item, and represents chiefly the payment in money of a former obligation to supply troops to the Government, and in some cases 'nuzzeranna' or fees on succession.

Expenditure. The expenditure account may, for purposes of convenience, be tabulated in the following ways :

NET EXPENDITURE, 1910-11.

Interest on Debt	£703,463
Military Services	19,265,042
Civil Charges	28,281,290
Famine Relief and Insurance	1,000,000
Provincial Adjustment	1,961,202
Surplus	3,936,287
	£55,147,284

(a) *Debt.*[1] When the management of Indian affairs was transferred from the Company to the Crown, the Government of India took over the debts of the Company, amounting to 107 crores ; and this sum has since been increased for several reasons, so that in 1911 the debt of India stood at 405 crores. The increase is due very largely to loans made for the development of railways and irrigation works. Though the Government has been borrowing money extensively for remunerative or public works purposes during the last few years, it has been at the same time paying off a large portion of what may be

[1] Government debts per head of population in various countries :

COUNTRY.	TOTAL.	PER HEAD.		
United Kingdom	£762,463,600	£16	15	4
India	270,063,145	1	5	0
France	1,070,437,700	27	5	1
Italy	522,837,000	15	5	1
Russia	934,249,600	5	18	11
Canada	96,747,400	13	9	4

termed the ordinary or unremunerative debt. The money which would otherwise have been used for the reduction of the ordinary debt has been spent on capital expenditure for public works purposes, and these sums are taken from the ordinary and placed against the public works debt. The result has been that the ordinary debt is only about one-seventh of the total debt of India. About six-sevenths of the present debt of India has been incurred by an outlay on remunerative purposes, the receipts from which more than pay the interest due. The rate of interest on the debt is for the most part at 3½ per cent. This is pre-eminently satisfactory, as many other countries, such as Japan, Russia, Turkey, and China, can only borrow money at a considerably higher rate.

(b) *Military Charges.* About 35 per cent. of the revenues are spent on defence forces and works, and this certainly represents a large sum of money. In the United Kingdom very nearly the same percentage of the annual income is apportioned for similar purposes, and all countries are spending large sums on these charges. It is the hope of all that the ever-increasing cost of armaments will in time be reduced, but unfortunately the tendency is to increase rather than decrease the amount. In India there is some cause for satisfaction in that great efforts have been made in recent years to reduce expenditure, that the proportion of money spent on military purposes to the whole revenue is steadily decreasing, and that the whole cost is defrayed out of revenue without having recourse to loans, as is being done in certain other countries.

(c) *Civil Charges* may be divided under four

headings and the expenditure in 1910-11 was as follows:

Collection of Revenue - - -		£6,114,457
Civil Services—		
General Administration	£1,756,260	
Law Courts - -	2,556,367	
Jails - - -	613,426	
Police - - -	4,196,239	
Ports and Pilotage -	31,359	
Education - -	1,662,607	
Ecclesiastical - -	124,678	
Medical - - -	919,225	
Political - - -	1,095,470	
Scientific and other minor departments - -	764,613	
		13,720,244
Civil Works - -	£4,243,629	
Miscellaneous and other charges -	4,202,960	
		8,446,589
		£28,281,290

The sum charged for the collection of revenue is somewhat misleading, as it includes the salaries of officials whose work is devoted very largely to other objects as well. The expenditure of the civil departments has been increased very much of late years, and this is due to the considerable sums spent on education, sanitation, and civil works. It must be remembered also that the revenues of the municipalities and local boards, which do not appear in the Imperial budget, are spent, to a large extent, on these objects. The miscellaneous charges include what is termed the "non-effective civil expenditure," such as printing and stationery, and pensions paid to retired officers or to individuals for political purposes.

(d) *Famine Relief and Insurance.* In 1877-78, the Government of India came to the conclusion that a form of insurance was necessary to meet the extra expenses and loss of revenue incurred in times of famine. It was resolved, as far as possible, to put aside every year out of revenue, £1,000,000. The money may be used either for the reduction of debt, or for the construction of public works, which would otherwise have to be provided by loan. Since the institution of this scheme, £30,000,000 have been spent out of revenues, either in the direct relief of distress, or in construction of public works, or in the reduction of debt. By this means provision is made for times of famine and distress.

A certain amount of the revenues must necessarily be spent in England, and these payments are known as "Home Charges." They are accounted for in the following way: Home Charges.

Interest on debt (remunerative and unremunerative) - - -	£10,760,746
Purchase of Stores - - - - -	1,025,455
Army Charges (Pensions, Leave Allowances, etc.) - -	4,617,294
Pensions and Leave Allowances (civil)	1,881,042
India Office and other charges - -	321,169
	£18,605,706

These charges are met in this way. Indian exports exceed the imports by a very considerable amount, and this involves a debt to India by the outside world, which is liquidated by purchasing bills on India issued by the Secretary of State. These bills are paid out of the Indian revenues. By this means two objects are attained with a minimum of trouble and expense. The debt of India to England for the charges explained above is paid, as also is that of the European merchants to India on the excess of Indian exports over imports. Sometimes the balance in favour of India exceeds the amount of the Home charges. The Secretary of State then issues bills in excess of what is required for Home Charges, and India benefits to the full amount by means of currency accommodation, or by an increased reserve to meet future liabilities.

Gold Reserve.

In the past, India has suffered very considerably by having to meet her payments in England in gold, whilst her revenues are collected in silver. The tendency in the past has been for the rupee to depreciate in value. At one time its exchange value was equal to 2s., but in 1893 it was only 1s. 3d., and there was a danger of a further decline. The position was as follows. With the rupee at 2s. it would require Rs. 18,00,00,000 to meet the Home Charges, amounting to £18,000,000, but with the rupee at 1s. 3d. Rs. 28,00,00,000 would be needed. India, therefore, would be losing Rs.10,00,00,000 a year through the decline in value of the rupee. The whole state of Indian finances, public and private, was in disorder. It was decided, therefore, to introduce the gold standard into India, and to give the rupee an artificial value of 1s. 4d. The Indian mints at the present day only coin such number of rupees as in the opinion of Government are required for public use. The profits of the mints on the coinage of silver are very large, as the rupee does not by any means represent its nominal value. These profits are invested chiefly in England in gold securities, which are put aside as a gold standard reserve. This is very necessary in cases of emergency. In times of trade depression the exports might fall off, and it would be necessary for India to meet her liabilities either in gold or in silver, which outside India would be worth considerably less than the statutory 1s. 4d. In such cases the gold reserve could be used. The gold standard reserve amounts to a sum bordering on £19,000,000, and it is now fairly assumed that the Indian finances are based on a sure foundation, and that no serious danger need be anticipated.

CHAPTER XI.

LAND REVENUE.

"At least £20,000,000 per annum is obtained in India by the land tax, but it would be as unreasonable to consider the amount as a burden laid on the people as it would be to consider that the whole rent which is paid to English landlords in this country (England) is an impost laid on the cultivator of the soil."

FAWCETT.

"What is technically called a 'Settlement of the land revenue' consists in the determination of the share of the produce or rental to which the State is entitled and in the record of all private rights and interests in the land." BADEN-POWELL.

"It is not in the Permanent Settlement of Bengal that the ryot has found his salvation; it has been in the laws which have been passed by the Supreme Government to check its license and to moderate its abuses." GOVERNMENT RESOLUTION, 1902.

History of Land Revenue.

It has been the custom of the Government in India from very early times to derive a certain amount of revenue from the land. In the laws of Manu it is seen that a proportion of the gross produce from the land was due to the State. In early times this revenue was paid in kind, and represented the amount of grain which the rulers considered their fair share of the crops. The system had its advantages in that the revenue was easily collected, and both the rulers and the cultivators received returns in accordance with the success or failure of the harvest. Under the rule of the Moghuls, however, the system of land revenue became regularized. Akbar and his Hindu Minister, Todar Mal, tried to build up a strong Government, whose authority would be felt in all parts of the country, and therefore established what is perhaps the greatest need of all Governments, an effective fiscal system. Land revenue henceforward was to be paid in cash rather than in kind, and a settlement was made as to the amounts due which would be in force for a number of years. A calculation was made from the gross produce of the last nineteen years, and one-third of the average crop was considered the right proportion due to the State. As the Muhammadan Empire fell into decay, the collection of land revenue became disorganized. The evil system of farming out the privilege of collecting the revenues became customary. These revenue farmers were in some instances the Hindu chiefs, whom the Muhammadan rulers wished to conciliate, or else individuals having some claim on the State, either by their position or by past services. They were known in Bengal as Zemindars, and in Oudh and Gujarat as Talukdars. As time went on, "the Zemindars did just as they pleased, and made the villagers pay whatever they demanded, or whatever they could extract from them." The actual amount paid by the Zemindars from the proceeds into the Treasury depended very largely on the bargain they had been able to make with the Government.

In his official writings, Mountstuart Elphinstone has given a clear account of the way in which the Mahrattas collected the revenues at the time immediately preceding the incorporation of the Peshwa's territories with the Bombay Presidency.

Elphinstone and the Mahratta system.

The central figure in those days was the Mamlatdar, who was in charge of a district, and under him were the Tarafdars, each of whom had charge of a number of villages; and in some cases there were important officials called Darakdars, whose business was to supervise the work of the Mamlatdars and prevent malpractices. The inferior revenue officials dealt with the village Patels, who settled with the raiyats the share each would have to pay. As time went on, changes of an unfortunate nature were introduced into the system. The office of Mamlatdar was put up for auction and sold to the highest bidder, who in turn would let his district out at an enhanced rate to under-farmers. All interested in the collection of the revenue, therefore, from the Mamlatdar down to the Patel were in league together to exact as much as possible from the unfortunate raiyat, and there was little or no check whatever against abuse.

Diversity of Systems.

As each province was brought under the control of British rule, the system of collecting the land revenue was so arranged as to suit the special needs and requirements of the province concerned. It has thus come about that throughout British India there are many different methods by which the money is collected, and, therefore, the study of the land revenue system is extremely difficult and complicated. Moreover, the duty of the British Government does not usually end with the mere assessment and collection of the land revenue. In many cases it does far more than this by establishing a record even of the rights and interests of persons other than the individual or the body with whom the settlement is made. The task before the British Government, therefore, has been very formidable. In the early days, undoubtedly, many mistakes were made, and the exactions in some cases have been excessive. This was the case especially in the Deccan, though the trouble was due to a continuation of bad harvests rather than to anything else. It has been the work of British administrators in the past, many of whose names are now forgotten, to evolve a system which may not be perfect, but at any rate is far superior to any that preceded it.

Official Organization.

The supervision over all questions connected with the land is placed in the Revenue and Agriculture Department of the Government of India, which was first constituted as a separate department in 1871. The head of this department has a seat on the Executive Council of the Governor-General. The land revenue administration is mainly in the hands of the Provincial Governments, and varies in different parts of India. In Madras, where there are no Divisional Commissioners, there is a Board of Revenue consisting of four members. Two of these deal with all matters connected with the land revenue, the third with settlements and the registration of land records, and the fourth with other sources of revenue, such as salt and excise. In certain other provinces, where there are Divisional Commissioners, the Board consists of two members. In the Punjab, the Central Provinces, and Burma all the duties of the Board are fulfilled by a single

Financial Commissioner. In Bombay, again, there is a different system. In that province the Divisional Commissioners, besides dealing with revenue matters, exercise a general supervision over the administration in the districts within each division. There is also a Settlement Commissioner and a Commissioner of Salt, Excise, etc. The unit of the land revenue administration is the district presided over by the Collector in the regulation and the Assistant-Commissioner in the non-regulation provinces, who corresponds with the chief revenue authority or the Government through the Commissioner. Below him are the Assistant and Deputy Collectors. Each district is split up into a number of divisions called Tahsils or Talukas. The officer in charge is usually called the Tahsildar, but in Bombay the Mamlatdar, and in Sind the Muktyarkar. In the office of each of these officials is a staff of accountants and inspectors, whose business is to keep in touch with the village officials and see that the revenue returns are in order. There are, as will be seen later, different types of villages, but in most there is an official headman or Patel, who has a direct or indirect responsibility for the collection of the revenue. The duties of the village accountant, called the Patwari in the north and the Kulkarni in the Deccan, are very important, and on him "depends almost the whole of the revenue management, past and future." It is his duty to keep the village accounts, to have charge of the village maps and registers, to render returns showing crops sown and harvested, and to prevent any removal or destruction of boundary marks. In certain parts of the Bombay Presidency the Kulkarni is often replaced by the Talati, who is an ordinary

Government servant and has no claim on a particular village. Each year what is termed the Jamabandi of the village is made, at which time the total amount of revenue due from the village is made out.

Zemindari and Raiyatwari Tenures.

Before referring to the methods by which the land revenue is assessed and collected, it is necessary to allude to the various forms of land tenure in India. It has been seen that at the close of the eighteenth century the collection of the land revenues was in the hands of revenue farmers. In some places, as in Bengal, these men have become the actual landlords, and are recognized as such by law. In others, as in Bombay and Southern India, they have to a large extent disappeared, or, at the most, have retained certain "overlord" duties; but instances of the Talukdari tenure in Gujarat and of the Khoti tenure in the Konkan are fairly frequent. "In the Madras and Bombay provinces," says Sir John Strachey, "the land is for the most part in the possession of peasant proprietors, with every one of whom the Government enters into a separate engagement. The tenure is called *Raiyatwari*." The same writer also quotes from the report of the Famine Commissioners of 1880 these words: "The tenure of the raiyat in Southern India is as simple and secure as well can be conceived. He holds his land in proprietary right, subject to the payment of the assessed revenue, which is fixed for a period of thirty years. He has the option of resigning his entire holding, or any individual field, at the end of the agricultural year. His improvements cannot be made a ground for increasing his assessment at the time of the periodical assessment. He can sell, mortgage, or let his land to any one without requiring the consent of the Government, and at his death the land descends to his children according to the rules of inheritance." In Northern India a different system of tenure, known as *Zemindari*, prevails. The village there is the unit of assessment, and, as a rule, the Government deals with the landholders. These men, who are called Zemindars, and in Oudh Talukdars, receive from the cultivators rent, a portion of which they pay to the Government in the shape of land revenue. In some parts, as in the Agra province, the village estates are held by small proprietors, who are associated together in village communities. In these cases, "the community is treated as jointly and severally liable; and the body regarded as a whole is, in fact, the landlord." The Famine Commissioners reported that "these Communities are represented by an elected or hereditary head, and are jointly responsible for the payment of the Government revenue due from the entire village. Sometimes all the land is held in common, and the proceeds are thrown together and divided among the sharers by village custom. Sometimes the proprietors all have their separate holdings in the state, each paying the quota of revenue due from his plot, and enjoying the surplus profits of it."

Baden-Powell and Land Tenures.

Mr. Baden-Powell, who is looked upon as the authority on Indian land tenures, has perhaps given the most clear and concise definition of these two types of villages. "The (raiyatwari) village contains a number of individual cultivating holders (who usually work the land themselves with the aid of their families, but often employ tenants). These holdings are separate units. The cultivators do not claim to be joint-holders of a whole area, nor do their holdings represent, in any sense, shares of what is in itself a whole which belongs to them all. They are, however, held together by their submission to somewhat powerful headmen and other village officers, and by use in common of a resident staff of village artisans and menials, who receive a fixed remuneration on an established scale, and sometimes have hereditary holdings of service lands." Of the Zemindari village the same writer gives the following description: "The important feature is that there is an individual, or a family (or a group of ancestrally connected bodies), which has the claim to be superior to other cultivating landholders, and, in fact, to be the owner or landlord of the entire area within the ring fence of the village boundary, as already existing, or as established by their own foundation."

The Permanent Settlement.

The land "settlements," then, may be considered with reference both to the zemindari and the raiyatwari tenures; and in the case of the former it must be remembered that the landlord may either be a single man or a group of men forming a village community. Another distinction must also be made. Some of the settlements are permanent and others temporary. The former exist chiefly in Bengal, and also in certain parts of the United Provinces and the Madras Presidency. In 1793 the permanent settlement of Bengal was established by Lord Cornwallis. The zemindars, who in former years had been the revenue farmers of the district, were then recognized as the actual owners of the land, but by the terms of the settlement had to pay 90 per cent. of the rent thus collected to the State. Some authorities hold that the permanent settlement has had most satisfactory results in that the landholders have been able to improve and develop their estates without any fear of their assessment being increased. On the other hand, there would appear to be grave evils attached to the system. An attempt was made at the time of the settlement to protect the interests of the raiyat. It was a difficult task, however, in those days to make a satisfactory survey of the land, and, indeed, none was attempted. With the increase of population and wealth there has been more competition for the possession of land. The rental of some of the land in Bengal is forty times larger than it was at the time of the settlement. This is due to many causes, the industry of the raiyat, the building of railways, the increase of population, the assistance of Government, and, in some cases, the development carried out by the zemindar; yet the whole profit goes only to the latter. The raiyat gains no benefit and the State receives in land revenue a far smaller percentage in Bengal than elsewhere. The permanent settlement has also been extended to the Benares district and to the northern portions of the Madras Presidency. The Talukdars of Oudh hold their land in an entirely different manner. After the annexation of Oudh, in 1856, these men were scarcely treated with justice, and, as a result, they were in rebellion during the succeeding year. Lord Canning was anxious, after the restoration of peace, to win over the landholding classes to the side of Government, and the Talukdars recovered their lost estates and privileges. The settlement, however, differed in many respects from that made with the zemindars of Bengal. The assessment may be altered from time to time; the land was carefully surveyed; and, fortunately, there is a record of the rights of all others connected with the land.

We may now turn to the other type of zemindari settlement, where the land is held, not by a single zemindar, but by a group of co-sharers, who are responsible for the payment of the land revenue. This method of holding land is most common in the Agra and Punjab provinces. Much more care was taken there than in Bengal, and the settlements were revised at first every few years. An opportunity was thus given for reconsidering the system, and, after a time, it became obvious that a survey was indispensable and a permanent settlement unwise. Most of the settlements in India are therefore revised every thirty years; but every encouragement is given by Government to the proprietors to make improvements on their property, and no increase in the land revenue can be made until the next assessment.

Raiyatwari Tenure.

The raiyatwari system exists chiefly in the Madras and Bombay Presidencies. The chief organizer of the revenue system in Madras was Thomas Munro, in the years before he became Governor of that province. Land revenue there takes the form of a certain proportion of the estimated *net* produce from each acre of land. In the raiyatwari districts a complete and regular survey of each individual field is an essential. In the Bombay Presidency a somewhat ingenious system is adopted. The revenue survey which was started in 1835 by Mr. Goldsmid and Lieutenant Wingate, was only completed in 1901. The land classification is not fixed in terms of the produce at all, but rather on the depth and texture of the soil. [1] "The comparative variations in the fertility of soils are expressed for convenience of handling in parts of a rupee, 16 annas representing the valuation of a perfect field, from which deductions are made for faults, such as slope or irregularity of surface, excess of lime or moisture, or inferiority in the character or depths of the soil."

During the rule of Lord Curzon the Government of India, with the assistance of the provincial Governments, made a prolonged investigation into the working of the land revenue system in India. Its officers, though in favour of extending as far as possible the periods of settlement, were opposed to the principles underlying the permanent settlement. They were of the opinion that the permanent settlement, as existing in Bengal, was no protection against famine, and that, moreover, it was the duty of the State to protect the interests of tenants living in that province against oppression at the hands of the landlords. The rate of assessment was also considered; and the conclusion arrived at was that over-assessment was not a general or wide-spread source of poverty or indebtedness. It was pointed out that a rigidity of system should be avoided; and that "a proportion of rent or of produce, which would leave a wide margin of profit in one part of India, might be vexatious elsewhere." In districts where land revenue was paid by the landlord to Government the rate of assessment has of late years been greatly reduced, and is now more often below than above 15 per cent. of the net assets. In the raiyatwari

Lord Curzon's Reforms.

[1] *Administration of Bombay*, 1911-12, p. 44.

districts the average assessment is very often below ten per cent. of the gross produce.

The inquiry referred to resulted not merely in a lucid exposition of the land revenue system under British rule, but also in certain improvements. The process of resettlement has been simplified and made less irksome to the people. Moreover, the revenue system in its early days appeared too rigid, and more flexible arrangements have now been made. It was found that an enhanced settlement sometimes bore heavily on those concerned, and a gradual and progressive enforcement of large increases has been laid down. Again, it appeared that as the assessment was fixed on the basis of an average season, the burden of a bad season was too heavy, the assumption being that the ordinary man rarely puts aside money in times of prosperity to meet payments in times of adversity. A system of suspensions and remissions of land revenue was therefore evolved by which these difficulties have very largely been overcome. A further change was carried out at the same time whereby the position of those affected by famine, sickness, or some other disability, might be promptly relieved by the remission or lowering of the assessment.

The present land revenue system in India is, therefore, a result of many years' experience and most careful investigation. Its main feature, both in assessment and collection, is its flexibility. Its study, therefore, is most complex and difficult, each province having its own particular system. The policy of Government in this connection is summed up in these words: "The true function of Government is to lay down broad and generous principles for the guidance of its officers, with becoming regard to the traditions of the province and the circumstances of the locality, and to prescribe moderation in enhancement, and sympathy in collection."

CHAPTER XII.

EDUCATION.

"I have often thought since I have been concerned with the Government of India that the first establishment of Universities was a far more momentous event and one almost deeper than the transfer to the Crown." LORD MORLEY.

"Many of the measures necessary for the diffusion of Education must depend on the spontaneous zeal of individuals and cannot be effected by any resolutions of Government."
MOUNTSTUART ELPHINSTONE.

"Ever since the cold breath of Macaulay's rhetoric passed over the field of the Indian languages and Indian text books, the elementary education of the people in their own tongue has shrivelled and pined." LORD CURZON.

"Education in the highest sense of the term gave way to the mere cramming of undigested knowledge into more or less receptive brains with a view to an inordinate number of examinations, which marked the various stages of this artificial process."
SIR VALENTINE CHIROL.

"I cannot believe that an examining University will satisfy any longer the needs of an advancing India." LORD HARDINGE.

Division into Periods.

THE history of the development of Indian Education under British rule can be divided into four distinct periods.

1. 1772-1818, a period of beginnings.
2. 1818-1854, a period when the foundations were laid and decisions of great importance arrived at.
3. 1854-1901, a period of rapid expansion.
4. 1901 till the present day, a period of examination and modification.

The relation between English and Indian history is very close, and it will be seen how events in England have reacted in India and affected its policy.

1772-1818. A time of War.

This is a period of constant warfare in both countries. England was engaged, first of all, in the war of American Independence and afterwards in the mighty conflict with Revolutionary and Napoleonic France. Reform, therefore, had to wait, and Pitt was forced to give up the three causes nearest his heart, peace, retrenchment, and reform, which have aptly been described as the beacons of his earlier and the will-o'-the-wisps of his later years. In India there were the wars of Warren Hastings, the campaigns of Cornwallis in Southern India, and the overthrow of the Mahratta Confederacy. The British Government, when not actually engaged in warfare, had perforce to spend its energies chiefly in strengthening the authority of its rule, rather than in extending the principles of progress. The first educational institution established by the British was the Calcutta Madrasa for Muhammadans, founded by Warren Hastings in 1782, and Government also supported the Sanskrit College at Benares, which was opened for Hindus in 1791, the object in each instance being to encourage the study of Oriental languages. Some years later, two forces tended to bring about a change of policy in educational matters, and to create a desire for Western, rather than Eastern learning. Christian missionaries arrived in India, and especially in the Madras Presidency, and began to start schools and colleges. In the next place, when it was seen that a knowledge of English was a profitable attainment, there arose among the Indians themselves a desire to partake of the learning and training of the West. The leader of this movement was Raja Ram Mohan Roy, one of India's greatest social reformers. By his efforts the Hindu College in Calcutta was started.

In England this was a time of peace and reform. The Napoleonic wars were over, and there was material progress in all directions. In Indian history there is a corresponding period of brightness, much of which was due to Bentinck, Elphinstone, and Munro. In Bombay, Elphinstone was keenly interested in the progress of education, and, on his departure, certain gentlemen raised the money to found two professorships in his memory. The lectures were given first of all in the Town Hall, but the fund was soon diverted to the support of a College, which still bears the revered name of Elphinstone.

1818-1854. A period of Reform

In 1833, Macaulay arrived in India as the first Law Member of the Governor-General's Council. At that time two schools of thought were struggling for mastery. Should the Government be content merely with giving encouragement to the study of Oriental languages, or should it try to introduce Western methods, learning and culture into India? The problem was as difficult as any that has confronted the British Government in India, and the controversy was severe; yet Macaulay took little time in coming to a conclusion, and within a few months drafted his now famous minute. His energetic defence of Western study, and his virulent opposition to the Oriental languages were decisive. With regard to the latter, he said that "the pupils will

Macaulay's Minute.

there acquire what was known 2000 years ago, with the addition of vain and empty subtleties since produced by speculative men, such as is already taught in all parts of India. The Sanskrit system of education would be the best calculated to keep the country in darkness. As the improvement of the Indian population is the object of Government, it will consequently promote a more liberal system of instruction, embracing mathematics, philosophy, chemistry, anatomy and other useful sciences." He goes on to ask "whether we can countenance, at the public expense, medical doctrines which would disgrace an English farrier, astronomy which would move laughter in girls at an English boarding school; history abounding in kings thirty feet high, and reigns thirty thousand years long, and geography made of seas of treacle and seas of butter."

Criticism of the Minute.

It is probable that in his main conclusion Macaulay was right. The exigencies of politics, the improved means of communication linking up East and West, and the actual desire of Indians themselves to be trained in Western thought rendered it impossible to adopt any other policy. "We are withholding from them," wrote Macaulay, "the learning for which they are craving; we are forcing on them the mock learning which they nauseate." On the other hand, many of his utterances were incorrect, and his condemnation of the Oriental writers was unjust as well as ungenerous. The opinion of Elphinstone was far more statesmanlike, and might well have been adopted.

"At no time," wrote he, "could I wish that the purely Hindu part of the course should be totally abandoned. It would surely be a preposterous way of adding to the intellectual treasures of a nation to begin by the destruction of its indigenous literature; and I cannot but think that the future attainments of the Indians will be increased in extent, as well as in variety, by being, as it were, engrafted on their own previous knowledge and imbued with their own original and peculiar character."

For better or for worse the die was cast; and the new learning was established. Schools and colleges were multiplied; and events tended to further education policy along the lines laid down by Macaulay. In 1844, Lord Hardinge issued a regulation enjoining the selection for Government service of candidates who had received an English education; and, secondly, "the adoption of English as the language of public business" rendered a still further impetus to the development of English education in India.

The Dispatch of 1854.

The period ends with the famous dispatch of 1854, written by Sir Charles Wood, the President of the Board of Control, to Lord Dalhousie, the Governor-General, and by it another important decision was made. Hitherto education had been confined almost entirely to the higher classes, in the hopes that they, as the natural leaders of the people, would spread their knowledge among the masses. This was what was known as the "filtration process" of knowledge, that is, knowledge filtering down from the higher to the lower castes. The dispatch, however, dealt with the education of the masses, and stated boldly "the responsibility of the Government towards the toiling millions, and its desire to combat the ignorance of the people, which may be considered the greatest curse of the country." For this purpose, Departments of Public Instruction were established, with a staff of officials to encourage the development of primary and secondary education. The dispatch also tried to remedy the more glaring defects of Macaulay's policy with regard to the vernaculars, in that it laid down that "English instruction should always be combined with a careful attention to the vernacular languages of the district, and with such general instruction as can be conveyed through that language." Finally, it paved the way for the founding of the Indian Universities.

This was a period of rapid expansion. At first, owing to the Mutiny and to other causes, little was done. In 1882, there were 7429 candidates for matriculation at the three Universities; and in 1889 there were 19,138. At first there was nothing but joy at such a wonderful achievement. "The thing must be seen to be believed," said Sir Henry Maine, "and I don't know which is the more astounding, the more striking, the multitude of the students who, if not now, will soon be counted, not by the hundred, but by the thousand, or the keenness and eagerness they displayed. For my part, I do not think anything of the kind has been seen by any European University since the Middle Ages, and I doubt whether there is anything founded by or connected with the British Government in India which excites so much practical interest in Indian households of the better class, from Calcutta to Lahore, as the examinations of the University."

1854-1901. Rapid Expansion.

Unfortunately, during this time errors crept into the system. The rapid expansion was quantitative rather than qualitative. As early as 1889, Lord Lansdowne pointed out that the number of openings which the professions offered for gentlemen who had received this kind of education was very small; and the fact that many of the graduates were unemployable was still more serious. It was reported that many of the candidates were becoming "mere machines of memory," and that mere powers of memory and cram were the chief assets for a degree in an Indian University. In 1882, Lord Ripon appointed a Commission of Enquiry, with Sir William Hunter as chairman. A long report of great importance was written after the Committee had visited many centres and examined witnesses. The most important recommendation was that as far as possible Government should withdraw from the direct management of higher education, which should be handed over to private, municipal, and local bodies. It is possible that the time was not ripe for so drastic a change and, further, the permission given to the managers of schools and colleges to reduce the fees will account, to a large extent, not only for the rapid expansion in numbers, but also for the rapid deterioration in standard, to which allusion has already been made.

Errors of the System.

The final period, which has been one of modification, began in 1901. Lord Curzon was the Viceroy, and he applied all his energies to educational reform. An Educational Adviser to the Government of India, known as the Director-General of Education, was appointed; a Commission of Enquiry travelled round India and issued a valuable report on the needs and conditions of the Indian Universities;

Lord Curzon and Education.

and in 1904 the Universities Act was passed. In 1911 the needs of education became so pressing that an Education Member of the Governor-General's Council was appointed.

Universities.

The Universities of India owe their existence to a Government Charter, and thus all changes in the Constitution require an amendment of the Act. The Governor-General is the Chancellor of the Calcutta University, and the head of the provincial Government concerned is the Chancellor of each of the other Universities. The executive of the University is the Syndicate, which is presided over by the Vice-Chancellor, who is nominated by the Government; and the other members, except the Director of Public Instruction, who is an *ex-officio* member, are elected by the various Faculties. The Registrar is an officer appointed by the Senate, who keeps the minutes of all Syndicate and Senate meetings, and is responsible for the transaction of all University business. In addition, there are the Boards of Studies, whose duty is to recommend text-books, and generally to supervise the existing curricula. The legislative body of each University is called the Senate, the members of which are usually nominated by Government, though a small number are elected by the graduates or by the Faculties. The Senate may pass resolutions connected with the work of the University, but these resolutions are subject to the veto of the Chancellor. At the beginning of this century, there were certain defects in the organization of the Universities. The Senates had become large and unwieldy, the number in Bombay being as large as 310. The result was that the policy of the Universities had not been kept abreast of modern innovations, and that reforms had long been due. In accordance with the Universities Act of 1904, certain changes have been made. The Senate of each University has been reduced to a maximum of one hundred in number; and in the election of members of the Syndicate provision is made that a certain number of those actively engaged in the work of education be selected.

The Act also dealt with such colleges as were affiliated to the University, many of which were in a somewhat inefficient state. Hitherto the University had been merely an examining body, which had set the standard required for each examination. By the inspection of the affiliated colleges the University was enabled to promote the efficiency of those institutions. At the present day there are signs that the University will take upon itself further functions and duties. Lord Hardinge has stated that a University which merely examines will scarcely satisfy an advancing India, and arrangements are being made to found a teaching and residential University at Dacca, which will serve as an experiment, and also as a model for similar institutions.

Inspection of Colleges.

The courses of study vary in detail in the different Universities, but in the main principles are the same. In Arts and Science the course is one of four years, in the middle of which is an Intermediate or First Arts Examination. The examination for the degree of Bachelor of Arts is held at the end of the fourth year, the same rule applying to the Science side. The rules with regard to honours vary. In Calcutta the honours and pass courses are separate; in Bombay the

Courses of Study and Examination.

honours student takes in addition to the pass three extra papers; and in Madras the honours course is taken the year subsequent to and in addition to the pass course. The degree of Master of Arts is given on a further examination, which takes place one or two years subsequent to that for the B.A. degree. In Madras the place of the M.A. examination is, to some extent, taken by the Honours Course. A Law degree can only be taken by graduates. There are other courses, such as those in agriculture, medicine, engineering, and the rule is that candidates for these courses should first attend an Arts College for one or two years before proceeding to the professional colleges.

Technical Education.

It is only recently that places for technical institutions have been established on anything like a large scale. There are industrial schools in many places, but the instruction given is often of an inefficient nature. Some of these schools are maintained by Government, others by municipalities or local boards, and others by private bodies. The most progressive institution of this kind is perhaps the Victoria Technical Institute in Bombay, which was founded in commemoration of Queen Victoria's Jubilee. The object of the institute is to give the students a grasp of scientific facts and to turn out workmen fit to be employed in any industry. Government Schools of Art have been established in the Presidency towns and at Lahore. The students are taught not merely painting, sculpture, and architecture, but also what may be termed "Arts and Crafts," such as pottery, iron work, wood-carving. enamelling, gold and silver work. There are also colleges of engineering, the oldest of which is the Thomason College at Roorkee, called after its founder, the Lieutenant-Governor of the North-Western Provinces in 1848. Others are the Sibpur College in Bengal and the College of Science at Poona. Students are trained for employment under private firms or the Public Works Department. There is also, as a rule, an apprentice department and an artizan class, where the instruction is very largely of a practical nature. The School of Forestry is situated at Dehra Dun, in the north of India. Considerable progress has also been made of late years in the Agricultural Colleges in the study of scientific methods; and there is a college principally for research at Pusa in the province of Bihar and Orissa. Attention is also being paid to the value of sound commercial training. Subjects, such as book-keeping, précis-writing, and correspondence are now being included as subjects for the School Final Examination, and at Bombay a degree in commerce is being instituted. Finally, there are the medical schools and colleges, which attract a great many students. At these institutions students are trained for the medical degree at the various Universities, and are in touch with the great hospitals where instruction in surgery can be given by the physicians, who are also professors at the medical colleges.

Moral Training and Hostels.

It has been the policy of the British Government to abstain from interference in matters of religion. In the Government schools and colleges no religious instruction is given; but in the aided colleges there is nothing to prevent such instruction, the only condition being that the secular instruction should be of an efficient order. Sir Valentine Chirol has spoken of "the careless diffusion of an artificial system of education, based none too firmly on mere intellectualism, and bereft of all religious and moral sanction." These are serious words, and others well qualified to speak have similar opinions. It must not be thought, however, that Government has been apathetic in this respect; on the contrary, much has been done to inculcate a better tone and to provide moral training in the schools and colleges. There are many Christian colleges in India, where religious instruction is given. Sir Syed Ahmed founded a college at Aligarh where Muhammadans are trained in the faith of Islam; and there is also the Central Hindu College at Benares. Many improvements have also been made in the hostels. Medical and other authorities have pointed out that at Calcutta especially and elsewhere the boarding establishments are such that physically and morally the students are evilly affected. In Calcutta, the University inspects these houses; and all over India better hostels are being provided by Government and private institutions.

Schools.

The provision and inspection of schools is necessarily the chief care of Government. The general policy of Government towards the schools has been summed up by Sir Andrew Fraser in these words: "The progressive devolution of secondary and collegiate education upon private enterprise, and the continuous withdrawal of Government from competition therewith, were recommended by the Education Commission of 1883; and the advice has been generally acted upon. But, while accepting this policy, the Government at the same time recognise the extreme importance of the principle that in each branch of education Government shall maintain a limited number of institutions, both as models for private enterprise to follow, and in order to uphold a high standard of education. In withdrawing from direct management, it is further essential that Government shall retain a general control by means of efficient inspection over all public educational institutions." Comparatively few schools, therefore, are Government institutions, the majority being in the hands of municipalities or local boards, of private persons, or of missionary societies. The latter may receive from Government grants-in-aid. In the olden days the basis of the grant depended upon results, but this system has proved unsatisfactory in India as well as in England; and the present policy is to allocate the grant in accordance with the general efficiency of the school and the amount of money it spends on the salaries of teachers, buildings, and general equipment.

Secondary Education.

Secondary schools are usually divided into Anglo-Vernacular and Vernacular. The former are those schools where English is introduced as a subject of instruction in the lower part of the school and as the medium of instruction in the upper classes. The latter are those in which English is not taught at all. There is a further division of secondary schools into middle and high schools. The middle schools teach children in the lower standards of the secondary course, and the high schools prepare pupils for the Matriculation and the School Final Examinations. As there are no Vernacular high schools in the Bombay or Madras Presidencies, the Vernacular middle schools are classed as primary schools in that they represent the highest point reached in Vernacular Education, which is marked by the passing of the Vernacular Final Examination. It is expected that a child will spend some five years in a primary school, and will then pass through the middle and high school standards. The matriculation may be passed by a clever pupil at the age of sixteen, but usually one or two years more are required to reach that standard. The number of candidates for the matriculation has grown enormously, and many educationists do not consider the courses of study prescribed for that examination suited for those who do not intend to proceed to a college career. In consequence, the School Final has been instituted, which necessitates a more practical training, and is intended to be a more satisfactory test of boys' fitness to take part in business life. In some provinces, also, as in Bombay, the School Final is regarded as the necessary qualification for entering the Government service.

Scholarships.

There is a systematic scheme of scholarships which assists any clever boy from the time he attends the primary school until he has graduated at the University; and even after that the Government, the Universities, and private bodies have funds at their disposal to assist a few students to go to England for the completion of their studies. There is a special department at the India Office whose business is to provide such students with all the necessary information and advice.

The Educational charges incurred by Government have steadily been increasing. In the first year of the century these stood at £576,000, but had increased to £1,539,000 in the year 1909-1910;

and since then considerable additions in expenditure have been made. The sums spent by municipalities and local boards are not included in these figures. The system of educational finance differs in the various provinces. In Bengal, the private or indigenous school, where the fees of the pupils are supplemented by a grant-in-aid, is the type; and in Bombay, on the other hand, the cost of most of the schools is incurred by the local boards or municipalities. The figures for 1909-1910 will perhaps give the necessary explanation (see p. 154).

Finance.

Education is subject to the control of the provincial Governments, but there is now an Educational Member on the Governor-General's Council whose duty is to superintend generally the work of the local departments. At the head of each department is a Director of Public Instruction, under whose supervision work an army of professors, inspectors, and teachers. There are the Indian Educational, the Provincial, and the Subordinate Services, the former being recruited from England and the two latter in India. The Universities, as has already been shown, are governed by their own organizations, but the Director of Public Instruction is an *ex-officio* member of the Syndicate and of the Senate, and many of the professors are members of the Senate and also of the Syndicate. For the purpose of the inspection of schools, each province is divided into divisions, each of which is administered by an inspector; and the Inspector of European schools is responsible for these institutions throughout the whole province.

Organization.

	Total No. of scholars.	From Provincial revenues.	From local funds.	From Municipal funds.	From fees.	From endowments.	Total.
		£	£	£	£	£	£
Bengal - - - -	1,433,523	332,864	75,757	9368	374,588	213,335	1,005,912
United Provinces - -	594,656	196,330	184,823	20,067	115,447	105,041	621,508
Punjab - - - -	299,436	124,064	82,633	22,865	88,930	71,067	389,559
N.-W. Frontier Province	22,378	3,878	6,061	3,539	2,993	4,331	20,802
Burma - - - -	414,748	113,550	27,133	22,675	91,801	29,575	284,734
Central Provinces - -	291,237	72,784	71,041	10,588	12,976	25,401	192,790
Eastern Bengal and Assam	904,690	129,101	88,253	3,429	156,287	62,531	439,601
Ajmer-Merwara - -	7,920	3,411	528	926	1,824	2,995	9,684
Coorg - - - -	6,335	2,021	789	58	827	359	4,054
Madras - - - -	1,126,084	260,452	76,340	21,126	232,602	205,432	795,952
Bombay- - - -	808,933	326,961	68,958	49,998	159,707	217,862	823,486
Total -	5,909,940	1,565,416	682,116	164,639	1,237,982	937,929	4,588,082

The provision of satisfactory and efficient teachers for all classes of schools has caused much anxiety to Government. The salaries given to teachers are often very low, and it is feared that the teaching profession does not attract men of such standing and intellect as would be desired. In Madras there is a Teachers' College, where a systematic training is given, and there is a degree of Licentiate in teaching, for which graduates are prepared. In Bombay there is a Secondary Teachers' Training College supported by Government.

Teachers.

The education of domiciled European and Eurasian boys and girls has also proved a matter of considerable difficulty. With the increased efficiency of Indian education these boys no longer control a monopoly of such posts as require an intimate knowledge of English, and, moreover, their style of living requires a larger salary than what would satisfy an Indian of similar attainments. "Every Viceroy," said Lord Curzon, "has gazed at this problem, and has been left sympathetic but puzzled." A great deal, however, has been done in recent years. A special inspector for European schools has been appointed in each province, whose duties are to allocate the Government grant between the various schools under his charge, and generally to improve the efficiency of the instruction. In most provinces there is a European School Final Examination, which in some cases is held as an equivalent to the matriculation. Some of the schools prepare for the Cambridge Local Examination, but the multiplicity of examinations is considered a serious evil. In 1911, a large donation was

European Schools.

given by a private individual for the improvement of European education in India, and the occasion was utilized for appealing to the general public, both in England and India. As yet there is no special college for these boys, and the Indian colleges, to which a few go after the completion of their school course, are scarcely suited to the training they have received at school.

Education of Girls.

Until recent years the Government of India has not done much for female education, and the Commission of 1882 stated that such instruction deserved special encouragement and liberality. But the difficulties in front of those who would make reforms in this direction are manifold. The supply of efficient lady teachers is very limited; and Sir John Strachey has said that "the idea that the women or at any rate respectable women ought to receive a school education, or any of the instruction that is proper for boys, is one that is entirely new in India, even among that small section of the population which has been powerfully affected by Western habits of thought." Much advance, however, has been made in recent years. There are schools, primary and secondary, for girls, and in some places the girls have taken their places beside the young men in attendance at lectures for the University degree. Whether or not a system of co-education, which is such a leading characteristic of American and other systems of public instruction, is advisable in India need not be discussed here, but the tendency seems to be growing towards the institution of separate colleges for lady students. An important school is the Alexandra Native Girls' English Institution in Bombay, which was founded in 1863, in commemoration of the marriage of King Edward VII. At the present time, in consequence of a suggestion made by the Begum of Bhopal, there is a movement to found a girls' school at Delhi in memory of the visit of the Queen-Empress in 1911.

CHAPTER XIII.

MEDICAL RELIEF AND SANITATION.

"The present state of living is deplorably low. Ignorance of sanitary or medical principles is practically universal."

UNDER SECRETARY OF STATE FOR INDIA,
SPEECH IN HOUSE OF COMMONS, 1911.

"The triple alliance of the rat and the flea and the mosquito has beaten the Government of India." GEORGE PEEL.

"I wish I could give a satisfactory account of the progress of sanitary improvement, but the prejudices and ignorance of the people make even simple reforms difficult. There are not many parts of India which are not liable to frequent epidemics of cholera, and in late years bubonic plague, which, except in the remote Himalayan districts, had long been almost unknown, has become lamentably destructive." SIR JOHN STRACHEY.

Difficulties in the way of Reform.

OF all the Government departments in India that of Medical Relief and Sanitation is perhaps the most important, and at the same time the most difficult. The conditions of life are less favourable to health in India than in Europe; and, in addition, the power of resisting disease is considerably less. Early marriage, which is customary in the East, has evil effects not only on the parents but also on the children of such unions. Good health also depends very largely on nourishing and suitable food; and in India the primitive methods of cooking add to the difficulties of digestion, and thereby impair the health. The poverty of many of the people also causes not only an insufficiency of food, but also of housing and clothing. The rate of infant mortality in India is alarmingly high. This is due very largely to the custom of early marriage, the ignorance of mothers, insufficient food, insanitary conditions, and to the fact that the mothers are often engaged in physical labours up to the very time of child-birth. Sanitary arrangements, even in some of the big towns of India, are very primitive, and in many of the rural districts they can scarcely be said to exist. "The village house is still often ill-ventilated and over-populated; the village site dirty, crowded with cattle, choked with rank vegetation, and poisoned by stagnant pools; and the village tanks polluted and used indiscriminately for bathing, cooking and drinking." The result of this alliance between a reduced power of resistance on the one hand and unhealthy conditions of life on the other is that the death-rate in India is very high and disease and ill-health very common. Still, improvements are being made, and it is not from want of effort on the part of the Government or its medical officers that the present situation is so unsatisfactory. At the beginning of the century the grant given to medical services was a little more than £650,000, and two years later the amount had risen to £900,000. In addition, the increased sums devoted to medical relief by the local boards and municipalities must be taken into account. Those associated with the big towns can also testify to the enormous improvements that have been made; and the efforts to combat the traditions of ages, the superstitions and the ignorance of the poorer classes, have not by any means proved a failure.

Medical Services.

The more important medical posts are filled by the officers of the Indian Medical Service, who are recruited in England by competitive examination, in which a number of Indians have been successful. The service was originally divided into three branches, corresponding to the armies of Bengal, Madras, and Bombay, but in 1896 these divisions were united. The medical service was started first in Bengal in 1764 for the purpose of attending to the servants and troops of the East India Company serving in that province. Though these officers hold commissions in the army, they are engaged very largely, as will be seen later, in the performance of civil duties. Their military duties are restricted entirely to the Indian army, as the needs of English troops serving in India are looked after by the officers of the Royal Army Medical Corps. There are, in addition, civil and military subordinate services, the members of which are recruited in India from those who have been trained in the medical colleges of the country, and have been successful in the necessary examinations. The senior members of the subordinate service are assistant-surgeons in the larger hospitals, or they may be in charge of smaller hospitals; and, in some cases, they may be promoted to posts usually held by members of the Indian Medical Service. The term subordinate service is used in this connection, but it corresponds very closely to the provincial service of other departments.

The medical administration is subject to the control of the provincial Governments, and the chief administrative officer is termed the Surgeon-General in Madras and Bombay, and in other provinces the Inspector-General of Civil Hospitals. In most provinces there is also at headquarters a Sanitary Commissioner, who is responsible for the supervision of sanitary matters throughout the province. In each district the Civil Surgeon is in charge of the medical and sanitary arrangements, and assists the local authorities in the management of their hospitals and dispensaries, but in Bombay there are a certain number of Deputy Sanitary Commissioners, who deal with matters connected with public health. The Director-General of the Indian Medical Service is responsible to the Government of India. It is his duty to supervise the medical work throughout India.

Organization.

Some of the hospitals in the big towns of India are more than a hundred years old, but, generally speaking, the provision of hospitals and dispensaries has been the work of the last forty years. In the past, the difficulties have been many. Medical officers were scarce; the Indians for the most part were unfamiliar with Western methods; and in spite of much generosity from private sources there was a lamentable lack of funds. Most of the hospitals are now subject to Government control. These are supported or aided by provincial, district, or municipal funds, and also by private subscriptions. Of late years the local authorities have taken an ever-increasing share in the administration of medical relief; and it is estimated that the local boards and Municipalities are responsible for 43 per cent. of the money devoted to medical relief and sanitation. There are also a

Hospitals.

certain number of independent private institutions, and others connected with public services, such as the railways and the police. In the Bombay Presidency, in 1910-11, there were 698 institutions working at the end of the year. Of these, 268 were supported from local and municipal funds, and 301 were private institutions; but the number of private hospitals in other provinces is not so great as in Bombay. At each district town there is a hospital under the direct supervision of the District Surgeon, to which the more serious cases are taken. In the Presidency towns are the most important hospitals, which are staffed to some extent by officers of the Indian Medical Service. The most important of these is connected with the Medical College, the professors of which are usually the physicians attending the hospital. At the Grant Medical College in Bombay the course requisite for a medical degree at the Bombay University is one of five years, and the students attend the Jamsetji Jeejeebhoy Hospital where the difficult operations are performed by the leading surgeons of the Presidency. The total number of patients treated at the hospitals in the Bombay Presidency in 1910-11 was 2,261,685, the vast majority of these being out-patients. There were 54,612 in-patients, and of these only 5,074 died, giving a death-rate of 9·3 per cent.

Hospitals for Women.

The medical treatment of women is a very difficult problem before the Government of India. The women of India, and especially those of the upper classes, are precluded by custom from attending hospitals where the physicians are males, and, in consequence, there is a great deal of sickness and suffering. In 1885, the

National Association for supplying Medical Aid to the Women of India was started by the Countess of Dufferin, and Lady Curzon and others have continued the good work. The Association is maintained by private subscriptions and occasional Government grants. In connection with the objects and work of the Association, the following words of Sir John Strachey may be quoted :

"Its object is the provision, on a large scale, of the means of teaching and training women in India to act as doctors, hospital assistants, nurses, and midwives ; the establishment, under female superintendence, of dispensaries and hospitals for the treatment of women and children ; the opening of female wards, under female superintendence, in existing hospitals and dispensaries ; the provision of female medical officers and attendants for existing female wards ; and the supply of trained nurses and midwives for women in hospitals and private houses." [1]

The same writer states that in 1908 there were 300 hospitals and dispensaries, and more than 2,000,000 women and children received relief. There were also 48 highly educated lady doctors, 90 assistant surgeons, and a large number of hospital assistants, while 507 women were studying in the various medical schools in India.

Surgery.

Surgery naturally takes a leading part in the work of a hospital, and in this connection remarkable progress has been made in India. The skill of the surgeons is very considerable, a fact which is proved by the success of their operations. In Bombay, out of 90,000 operations

[1] *India : its Administration and Progress*, p. 274.

performed in 1910-11, only 411 proved fatal, and the mortality among patients operated on was thus only 0·46 per cent.

Plague.

Since the year 1896 there has been plague in India. At first the disease was confined within the limits of the Bombay Presidency, but latterly it has spread to nearly every part of India. It is difficult to obtain reliable statistics as to the death-rate in India, but it is estimated that over 6,000,000 people have died from plague during the first ten years of the century, and the actual mortality is probably even greater. The most serious outbreaks have taken place in Bombay, the United Provinces, and the Punjab. Great efforts are made to prevent the disease spreading to other countries by careful inspection of outward-bound steamers, and these have in the main been successful. It has been discovered that plague germs enter the body through the skin, and are generally put there by fleas, which come from rats suffering from plague. Much progress has been made in the cleanliness of the houses and by the extermination of rats. Inoculation against plague has also been very successful, and statistics go to prove the truth of this statement. A few instances will suffice. At Belgaum eighty-three people, men of the Army Hospital Corps and their wives and children, were living close to the European Hospital, and were all inoculated with the exception of three. At the end of the plague season it was found that not one of the inoculated eighty had had plague at all, whilst two out of the other three had died of it. Of the police in Khandesh, 1508 were inoculated and 230 refused. There was ten times the mortality among the 230 uninoculated than there was among the 1508 who had been inoculated. Special inoculators are sent to the affected districts, and measures are taken to demonstrate the value of rat destruction, cleanliness, and inoculation in checking the attacks of plague.

Small-pox also is very prevalent in India, and principally in Madras and Bengal. It is a terrible scourge, and is perhaps the most infectious of all diseases. In England small-pox used to be rampant, but has been eradicated almost entirely by means of vaccination, which is almost universal. To be thoroughly effective, re-vaccination should take place every six or seven years, and also during epidemics of small-pox. In British India, during the year 1910-11, out of a population of 234,000,000, only 8,000,000 were vaccinated for the first time, and there were less than a million re-vaccinations. Still, the progress in late years has been very marked, in spite of many difficulties, and of the somewhat natural reluctance of the people to submit to an operation of whose value they are, unfortunately, ignorant. In the pages of the *Gazetteer* it is stated that during 1864-5 only 556 persons were vaccinated in Bengal, the United Provinces, and the Punjab; yet in 1902-3 more than five millions were successfully vaccinated in the same provinces. Each province has a large staff of vaccinators, who are maintained by the municipalities, local boards, or by Government. These men proceed from village to village, and vaccinate from the calf the people and their children. There is at Belgaum, in the Bombay Presidency, a Vaccine Institute for the preparation of lymph, and during 1910-11 over 600,000 doses were distributed through its agency.

Small-pox.

Cholera.

Cholera also is very common in India. The germ is one of those which gets into the body through the drinking water. Whenever there is a serious outbreak of cholera, special officers are sent to find out, as far as possible, the cause of the epidemic, and also to see that proper precautions are taken and that the sick are carefully treated.

Fever.

Fever is perhaps the greatest enemy of India, and it is estimated that between four and five millions of people die every year from this disease. Besides those who die, millions more are weakened and injured by fever. It is generally believed that the germs are carried by the mosquito. It is of supreme importance, therefore, that all stagnant water where the mosquito breeds should be removed as quickly as possible; and all wells and cisterns should be covered up. Government has done all it can to encourage people and especially those suffering from fever, to take quinine, which may be bought through the post office in small quantities at less than cost price.

Sanitation.

It has already been pointed out that in each province there is a Sanitary Commissioner and that the District Surgeon has become the health officer of his district; but in Bombay there are Deputy Sanitary Commissioners who supervise the work of sanitation and public health. Since 1888 there has also been a Sanitary Board in each province, which controls and supervises the work of the district boards and municipalities in connection with water supply and drainage schemes. In the Bombay Presidency, during the year

1910-11, the income of the district municipalities amounted to 92 lakks ; yet twenty-five of these were spent on water supply, drainage, and conservancy, and in other measures for the improvement of public health within the municipal limits. In the same Presidency there are local Sanitary Committees, appointed in accordance with the Bombay Sanitation Act, whose duty is to supervise the sanitary arrangements in the areas committed to their charge, to punish offenders, and to levy a small tax for these purposes. In 1910-11 there were 300 villages to which the Sanitation Act had been applied. The municipalities are enabled to borrow money from Government for big schemes of sanitary reform. As would be expected, the sanitary arrangements of the Presidency towns are carried out in a much more extensive scale, and these are controlled by the various experts serving under each municipality. The water of Bombay is brought from the Tansa, Vehar, and Tulsi lakes, which in 1910-11 provided the town with 6165, 3823 and 1302 million gallons of water respectively. Much of the improvement is due also to the Improvement Trusts in Bombay and Calcutta.

Medical Research.

The Government of India encourages the study of tropical diseases, and there is an institution at Kasauli, near Simla, where research is being carried on by medical experts. There are, besides, Government laboratories in other places where work of a similar nature is being carried on. In the Bombay Presidency the laboratories are located at Parel, in the building which once served as Government House. This is the plague laboratory for the whole of India. There is also at Kasauli and at Coonoor in the Madras Presidency an Indian Pasteur Institute for the treatment of cases of hydrophobia.

NOTE.—It is hoped that such students as read this chapter will have studied at school the *Health Reader for Indian High Schools*, written by Mr. Percival Wren.

CHAPTER XIV.

PUBLIC WORKS.

"No similar works in other countries approach in magnitude the irrigation works of India, and no public works of nobler activity have ever been undertaken in the world."

"When in 1844, I first went from Calcutta to the present Agra province, I was carried about a thousand miles in a palanquin on men's shoulders, and it took some three weeks to toil through a journey which is now accomplished in twenty-four hours."

SIR JOHN STRACHEY.

THE Public Works Department occupies a very prominent place in the history of Indian administration. This is not so much the case in England, where the railways are in the hands of private companies, the making and upkeep of roads and bridges regulated by the County Councils and Municipalities, and public buildings erected by private firms. The State only retains supervisory powers, which are carried out by inspectors acting in the service of the departments of State concerned. In India things have been different. In the past the people were poor and lacking in co-operation. In consequence, the means of communication were slight, there was little or no effort made to conserve the water and railways were few.

It was during the rule of Lord Dalhousie that

Government began to realize that the management of public works was a part of its responsibilities.

Organization of the Public Works Department.

Mr. Thomason, the Lieutenant-Governor of the North-Western Provinces, had already made a start in the building of roads, and in 1854 the Ganges Canal was begun. The first railway was that between Bombay and Thana, and twenty miles in length, which was opened in 1853, and in the following year another from Calcutta to Hugli was completed. At that time also a Public Works Department was formed in the provinces of Bengal, Madras, and Bombay, each being under the control of the Chief Engineer; and a Secretary to the Government of India for Public Works was also appointed. Since then, military have been separated from civil works, and are now looked after by the military department. The control of the railways, which was once vested in the Public Works Department, has been placed in the hands of a Railway Board, and is represented on the Governor-General's Council by the member in charge of the Commerce and Industry portfolio. Irrigation, buildings, and roads are in the hands of the Provincial Governments; and in Madras and Bombay the Governor himself usually holds the Public Works portfolio. At the head of each department there is usually one secretary for roads and civil works, and another for irrigation. With regard to the former, the tendency of the times has been in favour of transferring the financial responsibilities for ordinary roads and minor buildings to the district boards and municipalities. The Government of India also has a Public Works Department which is under the member of Council in charge of the Revenue and Agriculture portfolio, and has powers of supervision over the work of the Local Governments. As a rule, it only interferes in important projects requiring a large expenditure. For the purposes of administration, each province is divided into "circles," each of which is made up of a certain number of districts. A Superintending Engineer is in charge of each circle, and at the head of each district is an Executive Engineer, who has under him Assistant Engineers and a Subordinate Staff.

The Personnel of the Department.

In the Public Works Department there are three grades, known as the Imperial, Provincial, and Subordinate Services. In the former are the Chief, Superintending, Executive, and Assistant Engineers. In 1871, the Royal Indian Engineering College at Cooper's Hill, in England, was founded, the students of which were trained for the Railways, Public Works, Forests, and Engineering Departments in India. The College was closed in 1906, and the Public Works Officers are now appointed by the Secretary of State. The Provincial and Subordinate Services are recruited in India from those who have been trained in the Engineering Colleges at Roorkee, Poona, Madras, and Sibpur.

Finance.

The cost of Civil Works, which includes public buildings, is a charge against the Local Governments or, under certain conditions, the district boards and municipalities; and in cases where the estimated cost is above a certain amount the sanction of the Government of India is required. This arrangement is not possible in the case of irrigation, which for financial purposes is divided into two classes, "major" and "minor" works. The latter is a provincial charge, but the former, in that the cost must be met either by loan or from the fund reserved for Famine Relief and Insurance, is in the hands of the Government of India. There is an Inspector-General of Irrigation, whose business is to criticize the plans and estimates for irrigation schemes sent up to the Government of India, and to supervise generally the work of irrigation. When once the necessary sanction is given by the Government of India, the construction and upkeep are left to the provincial Governments.

Irrigation.

The Indian Governments have very rightly paid much attention to irrigation, and the success of their operations is equal to and even greater than that of any other country in the world. These works serve the double purpose of conserving the water and of providing an easy means of transit. Lack of water has always been a terrible obstruction in the way of Indian agriculture, but by means of irrigation nearly 38,000,000 acres of land already have been rendered suitable for cultivation, and on them most valuable crops are grown. Moreover, the rivers of India, except those in Bengal, are not for the most part navigable, but this defect can be partially compensated by the use of canals.

Wells.

There are various types of irrigation works in India, but they may be conveniently classified under three heads: wells, tanks, and canals. There are thousands of wells in the country which draw off the sub-soil water, and some of these have been sunk at considerable cost. Taken individually they are of comparatively minor importance, and only irrigate in each case land ranging from one to twenty acres.

This may seem a small amount, but wells of this nature are so numerous all over India that it is estimated that nearly 15,000,000 acres are irrigated by these means.

Tanks or reservoirs are used very largely in the Madras Presidency. They are formed in a narrow gorge between two hills by the construction of a dam or embankment which conserves the water in what looks like a big lake. The water is drawn off from the lower end by means of sluices, and is distributed amongst the surrounding fields. These works are often the results of private enterprise, but the Government has undertaken the construction of certain of the largest works and also the maintenance of a large proportion of all the tanks. About 8,000,000 acres, mainly in Madras, are irrigated in this way.

Tanks.

Irrigation from rivers by means of canals has been almost entirely the work of Government, both in construction and in maintenance. A weir is built across the channel at the head of the river delta and thus holds up the water which would otherwise flow down to the sea and be of little value to the country. The water thus stored up is taken away in side channels and distributed to the fields. This system is used very largely in the Madras Presidency. In Northern India a different principle prevails. The water is not so necessary in the lower reaches of the Ganges, as in that part there is usually a sufficient rainfall, but is urgently required in the United Provinces and the Punjab. At a certain part of its course the Ganges runs through a large valley, sometimes six miles broad, and also at a considerably lower level than the surrounding country. It

Canals.

is necessary, therefore, to intercept the water further up the river at Hardwar, where it leaves the Himalayas, and to bring it in what may be termed an artificial river to the watershed of the Doab, whence it can conveniently be conveyed even to distant parts of the country by means of canals. In the Punjab the waters of the Sutlej, the Jhelum, and the Chenab have also been diverted by similar means, the latter being a work of special magnitude.

Railway Administration.

In 1905 the administration of the railways was placed under a Railway Board, consisting of a chairman and two other members, whilst the Member for Commerce and Industry takes charge of the work on the Governor-General's Council. The Board is subject to the Government of India and not to the provincial Governments. The Railway Companies may appoint their own staff, but the Government of India enforces its right of approval in the case of the higher offices. The chief officer of each railway is usually known as the Agent, and under him work the Traffic Manager, the Chief Engineer, the Locomotive Superintendent, and the Store-keeper, who are in charge of their respective departments. Some of the higher posts are recruited from England, but exceptions to this rule are often made when men of necessary qualifications can be found in the country.

Railway Finance.

Towards the middle of last century the Government of India began to see the necessity of supporting the construction and maintenance of railways. Contracts, therefore, were entered into with certain companies in England for that purpose. Government granted the land free of charge and guaranteed the payment of interest at five per cent.; whatever profits there might be over and above that amount were to be shared between Government and the Company; Government had the right of buying up the railway at a fixed rate after the lapse of twenty-five years; and it also had the means of supervision over the management and working of the line. The companies concerned were the Great Indian Peninsula, the Madras, the Southern India, the East Indian, the Bombay, Baroda, and Central India, the Eastern Bengal, and what are now called the North-Western State Railway, and the Oudh and Rohilkhand. Undoubtedly the work done by these companies was of immense value to the country, but for many reasons the financial results were unsatisfactory. The cost of construction proved more than was anticipated, there was a good deal of unnecessary extravagance, the supervision was faulty, and, above all, the Mutiny threw everything into disorder for a time. In 1870, Government instituted a scheme by which the State should take in hand the construction of railways, and a fixed sum was allocated for a certain period of years. The new scheme, however, did not prove a success. Progress was painfully slow, and eventually the old guarantee system was again adopted, with certain alterations, which were to the advantage of Government. During the last forty years many companies have taken a share in the development of Indian railways under these conditions, and more and more money has been borrowed by the Government in the interests of the railways. The manner of raising these loans will be explained in the next chapter. Government has retained its right to buy up these lines thus guaranteed or assisted at the termination of a fixed period of time, and this is being done in many instances.

Much criticism has been levelled at the railway policy of the Government of India. Undoubtedly in the early days the contracts erred on the side of leniency, and there was also a certain laxity in supervision and some extravagance. The mere fact, however, that since the beginning of this century almost every year the railway budget, after deduction has been made for the payment of debt and working expenses, shows a profit, gives evidence of much wisdom and business-like capacity in the management of the railways. And, in addition, the examination of the balance-sheet is not the only test. In every country, and especially in one of vast distances such as India, the railways have increased very largely the wealth of the people. Lines also which could not possibly hope for satisfactory returns have been built in sparsely populated districts with the sole object of improving the means of transit, and of increasing the resources of those parts. Other lines, especially in the north-west, have been constructed primarily for military purposes, and from these losses must be anticipated. Above all, the great part played by railways in the prevention of famine is so important that it will be dealt with separately in the next chapter.

Success of the Railways.

CHAPTER XV.

FAMINE RELIEF.

"Land problems are the real heart of the politics of India. The truest test of a Viceroyalty is the degree to which the holder of the office has helped the people on the land. They are more than the back-bone of the country. They are almost the whole of India." LOVAT FRASER.

"Famine Relief administration is an arduous struggle to avoid extravagance on the one hand and mortality on the other." BAMFYLDE FULLER.

"What he (the raiyat) wants is the loosening of the bondage of debt which bows him down. Anything that will give him greater self-reliance, and teach him to look not only to Government or its officers, but to himself will be to the good." LORD CURZON.

Organization of Famine Relief.

CLOSELY connected with public works is the sad story of famine in India, and the attempts made in recent years to combat its evil effects. The ancient history of India is for the most part silent as to this terrible scourge, but from certain indications we can see that before and after the British first came to India the country has suffered from famine. The failure of the monsoon, the poverty of the people, and the fact that so vast a number are dependent on agriculture for their livelihood tend to bring about such disasters. In the past, very little was done to assuage the sufferings of the people. Lord

Northbrook realized clearly that famines must be expected from time to time, and that it was the duty of Government to frame a famine policy. Accordingly, a Commission was appointed by Lord Lytton, with Sir Richard Strachey as chairman, to make inquiries and see by what steps Government could help the sufferers. In subsequent years there have been two other Commissions at work, one under Sir James Lyall and the other under Sir Anthony (now Lord) M'Donnell.

In the light of the reports of these Commissions, and of subsequent action, we may try to learn the principles underlying Government policy with regard to famine. The great object of saving life and giving protection from extreme suffering may not only be as well, but, in fact, will be far better secured, if proper care be taken to prevent the abuse and demoralization which all experience shows to be the consequence of ill-directed and excessive distribution of charitable relief. Indiscriminate charity, therefore, has been avoided, and, as far as possible, the thrift and self-reliance of the people have been maintained. In times of famine in India every man has the "right to work," but not to receive charity. Lists are drawn up in every village of those who cannot work for physical reasons, and who would otherwise starve. To these a certain amount of grain is given. The children are given relief apart from their parents, and are given food and not money. A relief kitchen is started in the village under the charge of some responsible person to whom the children go every day for their meal.

Experience has shown that for the mitigation of famine, money should be laid aside during the years of prosperity. A sum of 1½ crores (£1,000,000) is set apart every year, as far as possible, for famine relief and insurance. This money is used either for the reduction of debt or for the prevention of debt which would otherwise have been incurred through loans for railway or irrigation purposes. In times of famine, therefore, the same amount may be borrowed without incurring any real loss to the State. Relief works, usually connected with railway construction or irrigation, are started, and provide the able-bodied with work. Very careful supervision is necessary, and certain conditions are exacted from the workers. The wages are small, but sufficient to give a bare subsistence; a good day's work must be done; and the works are situated at a distance from the villages concerned, so that all live near the works and not in their homes. By this means a sufficiency of relief is combined with a minimum of extravagance. Immediately the rains come the works are closed. All possible labour then is required for the sowing of crops. Relief works of a minor nature, and in this instance close to the villages concerned, are maintained in case of need. Advances are made to farmers for the purchase of seed and cattle, and everything is done to enable the work of the farms to proceed as quickly as possible. Remission or reduction of the land revenue is made during times of famine.

Relief Works.

Such, in short, are the efforts made to prevent mortality during times of want. The Famine Commissions have also made suggestions for the prevention of famine. Allusion has already been made to the construction of railways and to the irrigation works. The

Railways and Irrigation.

latter is a great preventive of famine, in that it gives a permanent supply of water, so that the crops may be saved in times of drought. The railways also assist very materially. The crops never fail throughout the land, and the ravages of famine are always confined to a certain area. Thus there is always a sufficiency of grain, if only it can be brought to the famine-stricken districts. This can be done by railways, and thus evils produced by want can be diminished.

Agricultural Departments.

The endurance of the people in times of famine is beyond all praise; and there are many instances of liberal help being given by private individuals. Unfortunately, however, the limit of their resources is not great, and a succession of bad harvests always brings famine in its train. Government has realized that it must strengthen these resources by other means. It has learnt to consider "the interests of the Indian poor, the Indian peasant, the patient, humble, silent millions, the eighty per cent. who subsist by agriculture, who know very little of politics, but who profit or suffer by the results, and whom men's eyes, even the eyes of their own countrymen, too often forget." Departments of Agriculture have been started, and these are controlled by the provincial Governments, subject to the supervision of the Inspector-General of Agriculture, who is an officer of the Government of India. The intention is to encourage a scientific study of agricultural methods, and by means of experimental farms to assist the farmers with advice. There is also an agricultural college in each province, and there is also an institute for research at Pusa, which is under the control of the Government of India. Much of the money for this establishment was given by Mr. Phipps, an American admirer of Lord Curzon.

Forests.

The Forest Departments were started as far back as 1864, and are under the control of the provincial Governments, the Inspector-General of Forests, who is an officer of the Department of Revenue and Agriculture, only having powers of supervision. Each province is divided into "circles" or divisions, each of which is administered by a Conservator of Forests. Admission to the Department is under three grades, the Imperial Service being recruited from England by men who have been trained specially in England and in Germany or France, and the Provincial and Subordinate Services being recruited in India, many of whom are old students of the Dehra Dun Forest College. There are about 100,000 square miles of reserved forests, and, in addition, about 150,000 square miles of what are called protected forests. The rules applied to the former are naturally stricter than those of the latter, but under certain conditions the people living near the forest can obtain timber and fuel for their own use. The forests are now worked at a profit. In 1909-10 the receipts amounted to £1,728,885 and the expenditure to £1,000,000; but the benefit of the public rather than the revenue gained from the sale of timber is the chief object of the Forest Department. In times of drought, cattle can graze within the boundaries of the forests and gain subsistence. The people themselves, in the last extremity, can feed on the roots and fruits that can be found within the forests. The protection of virgin forests is also a work essential in all countries, and other governments who are attempting a new policy of afforestation, often seek the advice of Indian Forest Officers. Much havoc is wrought by fire, and many men are employed to protect the forests from such disasters. It is also an undisputed fact that forests influence very largely the climate of a district. In wet places they act as a preventive against floods, whilst in dry and arid zones they tend to store up water and improve the fertility of the soil.

Land Alienation Act.

The constant alienation of land from the agricultural to the non-agricultural classes, and the hopeless indebtedness of the raïyats have also demanded the attention of the Government. In 1879 the Deccan Agriculturists' Relief Act was passed to prevent excessive interest being charged by money-lenders from agriculturists on the security of land. The result has not been wholly satisfactory; and the objects of the Act have sometimes been defeated by the evasions and chicanery of the money-lenders. Many years later the Government became convinced that the land of the Punjab was being alienated with alarming rapidity, and was passing into the hands of those who had little interest in its development. Those who had been dispossessed of their land were overwhelmed with debt, and were becoming a source of danger to the State. After great deliberation, the Punjab Alienation Act was introduced before the Imperial Legislative Council in 1900. The intention of the Act was to prevent non-agriculturists, such as money-lenders, professional men, and shopkeepers from holding land on mortgage for more than twenty years without the consent of the State. Lord Curzon himself stated his desire to checkmate the "Shylock who insists on his pound of flesh, and who, under the existing system, is in the habit of taking it in land, because it is the one security which his debtor can furnish." The Act was very unpopular in certain quarters, but there can be little doubt that the results have on the whole been satisfactory, and some relief has been given to a most deserving class of the community.

Under the terms of the Agriculturists' Loans Act, Government is empowered to advance sums of money, known as *Takavi* grants, to the agriculturists for the purpose of sinking wells, buying seed, and generally improving their land. These amounts are paid back to Government by instalments; and these instalments, like the payment of land revenue, are remitted in times of want.

Takavi Grants.

The above Acts have merely the negative object of preventing either the excessive charges of interest or the consequent alienation of land, but the Government has gone further in an attempt to encourage the agricultural population along the paths of co-operation and self-help. The co-operative movements in India have been most successful. Sir Theodore Morison has very tersely explained the difficulty in these words. "The cultivator must have credit; if it is hard to get he is ruined by the usurer; if it is easy he (borrows recklessly and) ruins himself." The constant indebtedness of the agriculturist is no new thing, either in India or in other countries. "Munro in Madras, and Elphinstone in Bombay," wrote Sir Frederick Nicholson, "showed at the beginning of the nineteenth century how utterly

Indebtedness of the Raiyat.

sunk in debt the raiyat was; nearly all the raiyats depend on the money-lender for maintenance from crop to crop; the whole of the surplus produced went to the money-lender as payment of interest; as for the payment of principal, it never entered their heads." In Germany "the poor were drifting into a state more abject than servitude. No longer did they rely on the play of their own personality. Their faith in themselves and such powers as they still possessed was fast waning. Their judgment was becoming warped. Their spirit of enterprise and initiative was losing all impetus." Mr. Wolff also bears testimony to the same fact in these words: "From one and all have I heard that selfsame, ever repeated bitter complaint that the villages are being sucked dry by the 'Jews.' Many laws, police regulations, warnings and monitions have all been tried as a remedy, and tried in vain." From Italy also we hear that the peasants were at the mercy of money-lenders, and were, moreover, compelled to buy inferior goods at ruinously high prices.

Co-operative Credit Societies.

Three great philanthropists, Schulze-Delitzsch and Raiffeisen in Germany, and Luzatti in Italy, took the lead in combating these terrible evils. Their solution of the difficulty was the formation of Co-operative Credit Societies, differing from each other very largely both in form and in detail. The result, however, has been the same. The peasant is gradually being emancipated from the thraldom of the money-lender, and throughout the countryside feelings of hope are taking the place of hopeless despondency. The peasant can now obtain the credit he needs, which will not put him at the mercy of the money-lender. This movement has been extended to India. The pioneer work was most ably performed by Sir Frederick Nicholson, a member of the Indian Civil Service in the Madras Presidency, who wrote a report dealing with such of these institutions as existed in Europe, and suggesting how the system might be adapted to Indian conditions. Such was the zeal of this official that after his retirement he returned to India to assist the people in carrying out his projects. Some years later, Lord Curzon caused the Co-operative Credit Societies Act to be introduced before the Legislative Council, which became law in 1904. The Act was cautious, and merely gave permission for such societies to be instituted, without laying down the definite lines on which they should be built up; and it also empowered Local Governments to appoint Registrars of Co-operative Credit Societies, who should superintend and encourage the work in their respective provinces. The result has been most satisfactory and each province has developed its societies in the way best adapted to the needs of its people. In this connection the words of Sir Theodore Morison may well be quoted:

"In Bengal the societies are all organised on the strictest principles of unlimited liability; there is no share capital and no dividends; the members of the society pledge their joint credit, and on the strength of it obtain capital from depositors which they lend among themselves. Membership is strictly confined to the inhabitants of one village, often of only one hamlet, and it is claimed that the Bengal societies are the 'humblest and smallest' collections of humanity that have formed themselves into co-operative associations in any part of the world. The Punjab is not quite so severely orthodox. There, a system of acquiring shares by instalments has proved very successful, both in providing the bank with capital and entrusting the active co-operation of members in the management. . . . The feature which distinguishes the movement in the United Provinces is the formation of Central Banks, which obtain loans on comparatively easy terms from private capitalists and large banking corporations; from the capital thus acquired they make loans to affiliated societies in the rural areas of the district. Other provinces have likewise special features their own."[1]

Such has been the success of the movement that in 1911, there were 3456 societies with a membership of 226,958 persons, and a working capital of £686,000. Out of that sum the State has been called upon to provide only £46,000. The rest has been found by the people themselves.

[1] Theodore Morison, *Economic Transition in India*, p. 85.

INDEX.

BIBLIOGRAPHY

'Imperial Gazetteer of India.' Vol. IV.

'India: Its Administration and Progress.' Sir John Strachey.

'Administrative Problems of British India.' Joseph Chailley.

'The Government of India.' Sir Courtenay Ilbert.

'The Indian Constitution.' Iyengar.

'Land Revenue in British India.' Baden-Powell.

'Government Resolution of Land Revenue Policy.' 1902.

'India and the Durbar.' Published by Messrs. Macmillan & Co.

'Report of the Royal Commission upon Decentralization.'

'Curzon and After.' Lovat Fraser.

'Studies in Indian Life and Sentiment.' Bamfylde Fuller.

'Indian Polity.' G. Chesney.

Lord Curzon in India.' Sir Thomas Raleigh.

Indian Speeches of Lord Morley.'

'Indian Empire.' Sir William Hunter.

'Speeches of the Hon. Mr. Gokhale.' Published by G. A. Natesan & Co.

'Education and Statesmanship in India.' H. R. James.

'The Empire of India.' Bamfylde Fuller.

'Rural Economy in the Bombay Deccan.' Keatinge.

'A Study of Indian Economics.' Chaps. XII. and XIII. Bannerjea.

'Report on the Administration of the Bombay Presidency. 1911-12.

'Statistical Abstract relating to British India.' From 1900-1 to 1909 10